# UNANSWERED QUESTIONS

## DISCOVERING THE TRUTH ABOUT JESUS

## Julian Pace

Carpenter's Son Publishing

Unanswered Questions: Discovering the Truth about Jesus
©2023 Julian Pace

Published by Carpenter's Son Publishing, Franklin, Tennessee

Edited by Ann Tatlock

Cover and Interior Design by Suzanne Lawing

Printed in the United States of America

978-1-954437-47-0

# Dedication

This book is dedicated to those
who yearn to know the truth.
John 8:32

# Acknowledgements

No book is ever really the product of a single individual and without the help of many special people, this book would have never come to fruition. Bobby Burgess, thank you for reviewing the manuscript and offering helpful critiques in numerous places. Your extensive training in apologetics enabled you to offer suggestions that made the arguments presented in this book much stronger. Dianne French, thank you for providing helpful and honest feedback when I was just beginning this project. Your input encouraged me to express my thoughts in more concise and relatable ways. To my editors Tiarra Tompkins and Ann Tatlock, your work on this manuscript was truly invaluable. You have both inspired me to hone my craft as an author. To the board members of Risen Savior Ministries, thank you for pushing me to write this book and publish it. Allison, my precious wife, thank you for supporting me unwaveringly while I completed this book. I could not ask for a more supportive and faithful life partner.

# Contents

# Introduction

Faith and belief is a tough and sometimes controversial topic. It comes with many layers, and sometimes even the most faithful of us have doubts. Have you struggled with your faith? Perhaps you haven't made the *leap* of faith because of lingering doubts. How do we know what is true? Many of us struggle, and many do so in silence. No matter what part of your faith journey you are on, I want to help you begin to seek and find the truth.

This book was born out of my own need to find truth. As I prepared for my ordination at a little Baptist church in the early months of 2014, I was having a crisis of faith. *"I believe that Jesus, the Son of God, rose from the dead after his crucifixion."* I can still recall typing these words on my laptop computer and most vividly recall what I was feeling at the time when I wrote those words. Never had I doubted more what I just wrote. *Do I really believe that? Should anyone believe these things, for that matter?*

I was preparing for ordination to the gospel ministry, was already serving as a pastor, and was also pursuing a master's degree at a Christian seminary. Despite my classic "believer" façade, I was experiencing a demoralizing crisis of faith. In public I managed to (mostly) maintain my composure for the outside world. In private, I was a deeply troubled person. Those closest to me (like my wife, Allison) could tell I was struggling. I dealt with bouts of depression, irritability, and sometimes even deep despair.

Before this crisis, my faith had always been a source of great meaning and stability in my life. I reasoned that if God exists as my faith teaches, then my life has meaning and the people around me matter. I felt assured of life after death because of Jesus's resurrection from the dead. If these core beliefs of mine were proven false, then the results of those beliefs would be false too. All too often I was in despair because my entire worldview was in doubt.

My life's stability was in jeopardy and marrying my college sweetheart and having a daughter with her made me realize that life was no game. Have you had that moment in your life that made things so much more real and all that more terrifying? Real life involves real people with real problems, real fears, and real needs. When I held my little girl, I began to ask questions like: When I sing "Jesus loves me" to her as she goes to sleep, are the words of this song really true? Was Jesus a historical person? Did he rise from the dead after being crucified by the Romans?

As a young man in the prime of my life, coming to grips with my own mortality was painful, frightening, and even debilitating. I knew I could not *live* long enough to learn or know everything. That was probably what made me doubt my faith the most. My life has an expiration date on it. I'm not going to live forever.

"*What does your crisis of faith have to do with me, Julian?*"

Even though you may not have experienced precisely what I have, you may have asked some of the same questions that plagued me.

Is there a God? Does life have any meaning or significance and what happens when we die?

Most people ask these questions in their lives at some point or another and they are questions worth asking. Socrates said it best, "The unexamined life is not worth living." This book was written out of my need to find real and solid truth. I eventually came to rediscover that the Christian faith truly speaks to the deepest longings of the human heart and mind.

No matter where you are on your spiritual journey, whether you are an atheist, a Christian, Muslim, Hindu, or someone who is not quite sure what they believe, this book can be a starting point for you as you begin to explore life's deepest questions.

While studying the evidence for Christianity's claims, I read very widely. I did not confine my research to resources written by committed Christians. Rather, I consulted many resources written by atheists, agnostics, Muslims, and a few of Jewish faith. In this most divisive time in which we live, it is critical that we learn how to engage with people and perspectives different from our own in a way that is polite and charitable. While I critique several non-Christian perspectives in this book, I have always tried to present these perspectives as accurately and as fairly as I am able. Relentlessly slicing through "straw men" for the purpose of scoring easy points for our side is not helpful in the least.

This book was born out of my crisis of faith. As I conducted my research, I wanted Christianity to be true, even while most of the time I very sincerely and strongly doubted that this was the case. I spent several years researching the answers to the questions, "Is there a God?" and "Are there good reasons to believe that Christianity is true?" As I journeyed for answers, I found there are good reasons for believing that God exists. My research also showed me that Christianity is true because its most central doctrine, the resurrection of Jesus, is supported by historical evidence.

My book is not the final, most thorough, or most definitive word on these two very important questions. Accomplished scholars from all over the world have asked the same questions that I have, done incredibly advanced research, and published books with highly respected academic presses on the subjects I am about to discuss. My book is merely the launching point for your spiritual quest rather than its destination.

Truth is an anchor. It can give us hope in a world over-whelmed by problems such as terrorism, social and political upheaval, racial injustice, pandemics, climate change, and the mental and emotional fatigue that often accompanies rapid technological progress. Life will bring us some of the hardest times and some of the most intense lessons. This book is meant to bring you more direction on your own journey of truth.

I wrote this book out of the conviction of truth that was born out of my crisis of faith. There is a personal God who loves us and his son Jesus Christ was born, crucified, then died and rose from the dead to save us. This truth has great importance for every living person. Coming to know the God of the universe and his son Jesus will radically change your life. It doesn't mean that bad things won't happen, it means that you will have the God of the universe on your side, standing beside you to face every good or bad moment. How do I know? When I finally understood the truth, that is exactly what it did for me. My faith in Jesus of Nazareth has given me hope in the very darkest of times.

Are you ready to search for the truth to these questions? Then grab a notebook and open your heart and mind to embark on this journey of truth, love and of course, hope.

# Chapter 1

# THE SEARCH FOR TRUTH

Have you ever been so consumed by your own crisis that you long to tell someone, anyone, just so the burden doesn't remain on your shoulders alone? In August of 2014 I could finally hang on my office wall a little certificate that read that I had been "ordained to the Gospel Ministry." I felt like a hypocrite. Here I was sitting in my office at the Baptist church that had ordained me, serving as a pastor, and I doubted whether God even existed! Some paragon of faith and devotion I was!

There was a large part of me that desperately wanted to share what I was experiencing with others, but what would my parishioners think of me if I shared with them just how much I doubted the core claims of the Christian faith? Knowing this about me, could they still have any confidence in me as one of their pastors? Would they even be able to answer any of my questions? Perhaps hiding what I was thinking and experiencing was wrong, but I did not know what else to do.

All too often we are buried in our own disbelief and crisis that we long to release it into the world. Perhaps we hope that release will bring us peace. In the midst of all that pain, I was just too prideful to share my doubts. The only person I felt comfortable sharing my doubts with was Allison, my wife. She was concerned for me, and she directly saw how my doubts were eating away at me emotionally and spiritually, but she never gave up on me or dismissed me.

God knows I didn't want my doubts to poison other people's faith. Despite my doubts, as someone with a pastor's heart, I genuinely cared about my parishioners' spiritual and emotional well-being. I wanted to share my doubts with someone besides Allison, but I simply felt I could not at the time.

Furthermore, while I genuinely enjoy the company of others, I am also a deeply private person. I have always been fearful of letting others see into my private world for fear that my struggles will weigh them down. Many of us fear becoming a burden to those we love. As that fear continued to put its own weight on me, I turned to books (a frequent refuge of mine) and the internet to find the answers to my questions. My intellectual and spiritual quest for deeper truth had begun.

Have you ever searched the internet for answers? You can imagine that it did not take me long to see a lot of ink has been spilled on the question of whether God exists or not! I was not surprised by the fact that there were many intelligent people out there defending the idea that God does not exist. Indeed, I earned my bachelor's degree at a

state university where many of my professors were atheists or agnostics, so this perspective was hardly new to
me. What did surprise me were the number of intelligent
and highly educated *Christian* people out there who were
making eloquent and reasonable cases for the existence
of God.

If God exists, as the Christian faith teaches, then life
has meaning and people matter. If Jesus really rose from
the dead, as the Christian faith also teaches, then we have
good reasons for believing he has given us a path to eternal life. If God exists and Jesus rose again, then the human experience suddenly becomes a vastly more hopeful
one. Before my crisis, I believed we have hope in this life
because there is a God who loved us enough to reach out
to us via the person of Jesus of Nazareth. Our lives matter
and there is life after death because Jesus conquered death
through his resurrection.

When you find your cornerstone fracturing, it is the
simplest thing to just believe you were wrong. Instead, all
these things weighed heavily on me. I seriously doubted my beliefs. "Are there any good reasons to believe in
the Christian faith?" So began my investigation of truth.
Did God really exist? Did Jesus really rise from the dead?
I reasoned that if there is a God, then life has meaning,
people matter, and immortality is at least a possibility. If
Jesus rose from the dead, then we have good grounds for
believing in life after death. If God does not exist, then
life probably has little meaning (if any), people may not
matter, and immortality is probably a pipe dream.

The realization of my own mortality made me think very deeply about what happens to human beings after death. I had always heard as a kid growing up in church that heaven awaits those people who believe in Jesus. Was this really true or is it simply "lights out" when we die?

Furthermore, Christianity does not demand that you believe in its central truth claims without evidence. I now believe there are good reasons to believe that God exists, and that Jesus of Nazareth rose from the dead. Faith in Jesus of Nazareth is *reasonable*.

As you begin this journey with me, I want to be sure you understand that this book is not meant to be a work of academic theology or history. I will bring you along on my crisis of faith journey and throughout this time together I will reference many academic theologians and professional historians. If my book does not answer all your questions or provide you with every answer, I can live with that. That said, I *will* introduce you to resources that can help you further explore life's most important questions. I will list these resources at the conclusion of this book. I believe them to be very worthwhile reads.

Now, in the interest of fairness, decency, and honesty, I must forthrightly admit that I do not write this book as an entirely objective researcher. Indeed no one, no matter how moral, fair, and charitable, can ever hope to achieve anything like complete objectivity. "We all see from where we stand" and I write from the perspective of someone who is a "cradle Christian," if you will.

As a kid who had grown up in church, I had implicitly believed that there was a God for as long as I could remember, but now I wanted to know if my experiences of God enjoyed rational foundation. For the first time in my life, I was *seriously* and carefully reading the work of well-educated, intelligent, and articulate Christians, many of whom were professional philosophers, historians, and theologians.

Furthermore, these same people were making reasonable arguments for the existence of God and the truth of the Christian faith. Being exposed to the work of Christians such as William Lane Craig, Jerry Walls, and Nabeel Qureshi refreshed my mind and my spirit and made me realize that the Christian faith might have more intellectual heft than I had previously thought.

The search for the truth was underway and I was not without an endless supply of arguments for both sides. If I was going to find the truth, I was going to need to truly read, research, and read some more. Books and articles of all kinds from atheist authors to spirit-filled Christian authors. There was no ground I was unwilling to cover. The hunt was on.

# Chapter 2

# THE EXISTENCE OF
# UNIVERSAL MORAL LAWS

Are you a good person? So often when we think of our lives on a surface level, most of us believe ourselves to be good. To an extent, I would say you are correct. Do you always do the right thing? That question begins the conversation that in order to say you always do the right thing, we must first determine what is right and what is wrong. In that is the beginning of our journey to determine if Moral Truths really exist.

As I began this truth journey, I was deeply surprised by just how *many* highly sophisticated philosophical arguments for God's existence Christian thinkers had formulated over the centuries. Thinkers like Thomas Aquinas, William Paley, Alvin Plantinga, Norman Geisler, Jerry Walls, David Baggett, and William Lane Craig had all produced persuasive philosophical arguments demonstrating that God is the best explanation for the existence of the cosmos and moral values.

Indeed, if I were to present all the arguments in favor of God's existence that have been produced over the centuries, this book would be very long. (And perhaps a little boring!) For this reason, I will focus on what most scholars call the "moral argument" for God's existence because it is the argument that I personally found the most impactful when conducting my research. On an experiential level, this argument resonated most deeply with me as a person.

My first exposure to the moral argument came from reading C.S Lewis's *Mere Christianity*. It wasn't my first read through as I had read *Mere Christianity* in college long before my crisis of faith began. However, while I found Lewis's reasoning impressive and his writing style engaging, the book did not make a lasting impression on me at first. I was far more concerned with my music back in those days. My biggest goal was to be a folk singer in the vein of John Denver; I even had the long hair to boot! When I read *Mere Christianity* the first time, I thought that Christianity was just obviously true. Who could reasonably doubt that the incomparable Jesus of Nazareth was really the Savior of the world? Only later would that book make a deeper impression on me and aid me in my quest for deeper truth.

In *Mere Christianity*, Lewis debates that every society both past and present has showed some understanding of right and wrong. Lewis notes that codes of morality from different cultures can often differ substantially in terms of their details and emphases. As with many things in our world, we notice the differences first. We also have to remember that our differences lead us to see the many important similarities as well. To demonstrate his point, Lewis presents it this way:

> I know that some people say the idea of a Law of Nature or decent behavior known to all men is unsound, because different civilizations and different ages have had quite different moralities. But this is not true. There have been differences between their moralities, but these have never amounted to anything like a total difference. If anyone will take the trouble to compare the moral teaching of, say, the ancient Egyptians, Babylonians, Hindus, Chinese, Greeks and Romans, what will really strike him will be how very alike they are to each other and our own ... Think of a country where people were admired for running away in battle, or where a man felt proud of double-crossing all the people who had been kindest to him. You might just as well try to imagine a country where two and two make five.[1]

Let me illustrate Lewis's point from another angle. Many, if not all of us, were taught in school about the events that transpired during the Holocaust. If you asked everyone you know, you would be hard pressed to find someone who would argue that the events of the Holocaust were morally right. Sure, you might find the odd (and gravely mistaken) person who denies that the Holocaust took place. In that case, I think it is safe to say a person who tries to defend the atrocities of the Holocaust,

1. C.S. Lewis, *Mere Christianity* (New York: Touchstone, 1996), 19.

many of which were perpetrated against innocent children as well as racial and ethnic minorities, is grossly morally deficient.

Do you believe there is an internal compass directing us to right or wrong? The evidence from history and the study of other cultures, and perhaps ever more importantly, our own experience, suggests that human beings (almost universally) have a sense of right and wrong. Some things are so cruel, so unloving, so dishonorable that no sane person should ever consider doing them. Although the specificities of moral codes differ from culture to culture, all cultures hold to some sort of moral code. In the end, human beings appear hopelessly moral, perhaps even in spite of ourselves.

Throughout all recorded history, in some way, there has always been a sense of morality. This fact has led many people, including Lewis, professional philosophers such as Jerry Walls and David Baggett, and (of course) myself, to ask this important question: *Why?* Why is it that human beings from many different cultures and backgrounds tend to sense that certain things are morally right and morally wrong? What explanation can we give for the experience of moral perception common to most human beings?

Lewis's answer to this question is, "The existence of a code of morality in every culture strongly implies the existence of a transcendent moral lawgiver."

Namely, God.

# Chapter 3

# FUNDAMENTAL MORALITY

## DO OBJECTIVE MORAL TRUTHS REALLY EXIST?

What are objective moral truths? Every culture recognizes a distinction between right and wrong. This suggests there is a larger reality that we are all connected to in some way. If every culture makes a distinction between things that are right to do and things that are wrong to do, is it possible that some actions are wrong regardless of cultural context? For example, rape of another human being is wrong whether the crime itself is committed in ancient China or 21st-century America. Furthermore, remembering that every culture makes a distinction between right and wrong, is it possible that this reality points to the existence of certain "objective moral truths" that all people should live by?

J.B. Phillips, an Anglican clergyman, puts it this way, "Why is there this almost universal moral sense? Why do we consider that 'good' is a better thing than 'evil'? Surely this recognition of good, so deeply rooted and so universal, is another far from negligible pointer to Reality."[2] Human beings can intuit the difference between right and wrong (albeit often imperfectly) because we are in some sense a reflection of God himself. God has designed us to discern the difference between right and wrong. God has given people a conscience.

All expressions of Christianity (Protestant, Orthodox, and Roman Catholic) teach that we as human beings are made in "God's image." Simply put, this idea expresses that, like God, people can reason, be creative, make moral judgements, and have the capacity for relationships.

When I speak of "objective moral truths," what I mean to denote is the idea that there are certain moral realities, standards, and responsibilities that apply to every human being regardless of the time or culture in which they live, and they exist because they proceed from God's very nature. We are reminded of them and compelled to conform to their standards by our own conscience. The person who argues for the existence of objective moral truths would argue that crimes like rape of another human being are never justified regardless of cultural circumstances. I think most people would agree with this statement: "Rape of another human being is never justified." If you can affirm the previous statement,

2. J.B. Phillips, *Your God is Too Small* (New York: Macmillan, 1979), 71.

then you have just affirmed the existence of objective moral truths.

## THE ARGUMENT

Objective moral truths exist. There is a distinct difference between things that are morally good and morally bad. God is by far the best explanation, and foundation for, the existence of objective moral truths. The simple conclusion is that God exists. That is, unless we can recommend a far better explanation for the existence of objective moral truths.

Now, many people have objected to the argument I have just presented. "Are you saying that for me to be a good person I have to believe in God? What a dismissive and extremely arrogant thing to say! I'm an atheist, I'm kind to other people, I treat other people with dignity, I donate to various charities." In response to this I would agree and say, "Yes, it would be dismissive and arrogant of me to think that atheists can't be good people or do good things. However, that is not what I am saying." The argument I have just presented for God's existence does not say that to be a good person you have to believe in God's existence. I have known many nonreligious people who live morally exemplary lives. Atheists do good things and live decent lives every day. I also

IF OBJECTIVE MORAL TRUTHS REALLY DO EXIST, THEN WE OUGHT TO BE ABLE TO PROVIDE A RESPONSIBLE AND RATIONAL EXPLANATION FOR THEIR EXISTENCE.

know Christians who live the opposite of what they "say" their belief system is.

The argument I have presented *is* saying that if objective moral truths really do exist, then we ought to be able to provide a responsible and rational explanation for their existence, and I am convinced that the best explanation for their existence is that there is a transcendent moral lawgiver. Namely, God. To demonstrate that the moral argument is false, we must either deny that objective moral truths exist—that is, there is no real difference between doing what we call "good things or evil things,"—or we could try to deny that God is the best explanation of the existence of objective moral truths and provide an alternative explanation for their existence. I will consider some objections to their existence now.

The opposing argument for the lack of God's existence is that objective moral truths do not exist. Sure, human beings may *perceive* some things as being right and wrong, but such moral truths do not really exist. They are simply constructs of our own making or a byproduct of our evolutionary development to ensure the human race's survival. Some people might call this a kind of "herd morality." To determine whether the position of "moral nihilism" (objective moral truths do not exist) is true, we will follow the assumptions of moral nihilism to their logical conclusions. We will do this by way of two examples.

Let me introduce you to a lady named Irena Sendler. Sendler was a social worker in Poland during the Second World War. During that time, the Nazis instructed her to go to work in the Warsaw Ghetto to confirm whether a typhus outbreak was imminent. Though the Nazis were ultimately unconcerned about the health of the Jewish people who had been forced to live there, they did fear that if typhus broke out in the Ghetto then it could spread to the larger German population. While working in the Ghetto, Sendler began to feel compassion for the Jewish people and their plight in the squalid conditions of the Ghetto.

Despite her difficult assignment she saw an opportunity. Sendler began to smuggle into the Ghetto food, clothing, and medicine to help the Jews who were living there. Later when the Nazis began exporting people to the concentration camps of Auschwitz, Buchenwald, and Dachau, she began to smuggle children to safety outside of the Ghetto. Although the Nazis eventually discovered her activities and punished her severely for her efforts, she managed to save the lives of many children. She is rightly remembered as a hero.

Allow me to introduce you to another person: Heinrich Himmler. Himmler was appointed by the dictator of Nazi Germany, Adolf Hitler. His job was to rid Germany of the so-called "Jewish problem." Himmler is probably more directly responsible for the Holocaust than any other individual in history. Due to his actions, over six million Jews, Romani, disabled persons, dissidents, and many other unfortunate people were either worked to death in concentration camps or were sentenced to death in the gas chambers. The Holocaust is rightly remembered as one of the greatest crimes against humanity ever committed. Few people who visit the Holocaust Museum in

Washington D.C., or the concentration camps themselves at Auschwitz, Buchenwald, and Dachau can leave without being emotionally, and often quite visibly, moved.

Why share examples of two people who led such radically different lives? For the sake of comparison. The moral nihilist is forced into the conclusion, due to their rejection of the existence of objective moral truths, that the actions of Irena Sendler and Heinrich Himmler are objectively no different. If we accept moral nihilism, then the difference between right and wrong becomes a matter of mere personal preference. Not unlike the difference between my favorite color being blue and my wife's favorite being green, or someone preferring strawberry ice cream and your friend preferring chocolate ice cream.

Are we really prepared to accept the awful conclusions of moral nihilism, swallow hard, and say that the actions of Irena Sendler and Heinrich Himmler were objectively no different? Can we really live with such a notion? Can society, at least a happy and hopeful one, exist on such a foundation? How do we not succumb entirely to despair if moral nihilism is really true?

Noted Christian apologist and professional philosopher William Lane Craig points out in his book *On Guard* that even though many people are prepared to argue on an intellectual level that objective moral truths do not exist, they still make moral judgements about good and bad behavior quite frequently. Many moral nihilists still live as though objective moral truths are a reality. In this regard they behave inconsistently with their worldview. In his book, Craig cites the example of the famous atheist Richard Dawkins (formerly a professor at Oxford University) to demonstrate that even the most committed moral nihilist cannot live consistently with the conclusions of their own worldview.

> For although he [Richard Dawkins] says that there is no evil, no good, nothing but pitiless indifference, he is an unabashed moralist. He vigorously condemns such actions as the harassment and abuse of homosexuals, religious indoctrination of children, the Incan practices of human sacrifice, and prizing cultural diversity over the interests of Amish children. He even goes so far as to offer his own amended Ten Commandments for guiding moral behavior, all the while marvelously oblivious to the contradiction with his ethical subjectivism.[3]

Craig demonstrates that while someone can *rationally* hold to, and defend, moral nihilism, few (if anyone) can *live* with its consequences and corollaries. Thus, while the moral nihilist *rationally* affirms that objective moral truths do not exist, they live as if they do. The conclusions of moral nihilism are just too terrible to live with, so the moral nihilist often chooses (subconsciously or otherwise) to live inconsistently instead.

As I reflected on some of my experiences while studying at a state university a few years prior, Craig's argument really resonated for me. I remember one of my English

---

3. William Lane Craig, *On Guard: Defending Your Faith with Reason and Precision* (Colorado Springs: David C. Cook, 2010), 43.

professors stated publicly in a lecture that she held to a broadly "postmodern" worldview. Postmodernism is an ideology that says morality is subjective, conditional, and entirely dependent on cultural context. For example, while in western societies men and women (ideally) enjoy civil liberties in equal measure, this same arrangement may not exist everywhere. Westerners have little right to criticize such an arrangement. Equal access to civil liberties may be a moral good in the West, but not necessarily everywhere else.

Fundamentally, postmodernism denies that objective moral truths really exist, and yet, this very same professor who wore her postmodern convictions so very clearly on her sleeve, regularly made us read books that dealt with themes of female subjugation and its negative impact on society. This professor (quite rightly!) regularly and severely criticized men who prey on women and use their superior physical strength and positions of influence to intimidate women and advance their own interests and pleasure.

To hammer home her point she would often utilize examples from non-Western contexts. Yet this professor was quite ready to say that morality is culturally conditional and fluid and yet she also was equally clear in her condemnation of the subjugation of women, regardless of cultural context! My still developing mind sensed on some level that her worldview was problematic. It was surprising that she could not see the blatant contradiction herself. In class discussions, I might have pointed out more sharply her lack of consistency but back then I was more concerned with simply passing her class (I was not exactly a star student back in those days and as they say, "Cs get degrees.")

It would seem that we are faced with the stubborn fact that something moral tugs at the human person deep down inside. Human beings are hopelessly moral. Sure, we may disagree about the details of how people should live but most of us would agree that there is a clear moral distinction between loving or hating your fellow human beings. The thought of a world where there is no difference between the two would be a kind of hell on earth.

# Chapter 4

# ACKNOWLEDGING THE EXISTENCE OF GOOD AND EVIL

History has provided humanity many examples of good and evil. The earth is littered with the monuments that have been erected to encourage learning from what has happened in the past. All too often, we think that humanity doesn't need the reminders. Yet, despite the reminders, history continues to repeat itself. Why? It is simply because good and evil both exist, and it is the acknowledgment of the two and the rebuttal of moral nihilism that we are going to tackle in this chapter.

The easiest way for humans to learn anything is through experience. You can talk about something all day long, but if the other person has never had similar experiences, it becomes a story that they may or may not attempt to relate to. My first experience of the very real existence of good and evil happened on September 11, 2001. No matter your age, this is a date that in fact lives in infamy. As a child of the 90s, the terrorist attack on the twin towers of the World Trade Center is one of my most vivid memories. With bated breath, the entire country sat at the edge of their seats. As video footage of the first tower, in flames, filtered through the news, we watched as a plane flew into the second tower live on national television.

Watching news coverage of the event and seeing how the adults around me reacted to what was happening is an experience that is hard to describe. Seeing the ash-covered citizens running down the street as the towers collapsed. Hearing the stories of the suffering of survivors and of families who had lost loved ones. Over the days to come, there would be pictures and videos of people who jumped from the towers out of sheer desperation. Back then, I knew nothing about the geopolitical situation that led to the terrorist attack. But I did know this. Evil creates human suffering. Suffering that no human being deserves to experience. Evil and good are distinct and they truly exist.

EVIL CREATES HUMAN SUFFERING.

"Pastor Julian, what does this have to do with objective moral truths?" I am so glad you asked. Objective moral truths are deeply connected to good and evil because it is the mere existence of both that helps prove their existence! Think about your own experiences. When faced with the terrors of human suffering we are (rightly) filled with empathy, compassion, and sometimes even righteous anger. I do not think we should lightly set aside what our own experience seems to confirm so very clearly. Human conscience continually reasserts itself and suggests very strongly to us that there is a clear distinction between good and evil.

Now a few people, such as thinkers like Bertrand Russell, have argued that moral nihilism (the nonexistence of objective moral truths) is inescapable, and we must somehow learn to live with this terrible fact. Indeed, the moral nihilist asks, "Do we really have any good reasons for believing that objective moral truths really exist?" In response to this I would argue that we are justified in believing that they exist unless we are given very compelling reasons that show they do not exist. Indeed, the conclusions of moral nihilism are just too horrific to accept if there is another viable alternative. Furthermore, and quite importantly, the global consensus seems to confirm that terrorism, rape, murder, and child abuse are all morally wrong.

Our conscience simply seems to scream out to us that no person should be subjected to the injustices I have just mentioned. Something to the very core of our humanity tells us that some things are simply objectively morally wrong, and no sane person should ever consider doing them. Indeed, unless our faculties are somehow shown to be defective, then we should trust them when our conscience affirms the distinct difference between things which are right and things which are wrong.

Perhaps there are some who might respond that we should not be carried away too quickly by this line of reasoning. Indeed, some have argued that human beings only make distinctions between right and wrong because we have been conditioned to do so by the slow process of human evolution. That the process of biological evolution has programmed into us certain behaviors and thought patterns that help ensure our species' survival. For example, we sense it is wrong to murder or steal simply because such behaviors are bad for the flourishing of the human species. When we make distinctions between right and wrong, our evolutionary programming is simply kicking in to help us distinguish between "helpful" and "unhelpful" behaviors. Objective moral truths don't really exist, we just think they do because a kind of "herd morality" has become so deeply engrained in us due to the slow process of human evolution and development.

While this argument is a rather common one, it is problematic for several reasons. Its greatest failing is it commits what philosophers call the "genetic fallacy." The genetic fallacy is when someone tries to disprove a belief by simply demonstrating how someone came to hold it. For example, I might believe the Nazis did morally objectionable things simply because they were negatively portrayed in the film *Saving Private Ryan*. While in many ways a realistic portrayal of combat during World War II, it is ultimately a work of fiction. While the origin of my belief is surely problematic (forming historical and moral judgements from a popular Hollywood film is probably unwise!) it does not change the fact that what I believe is still true!

Now before you get out your pitchforks and torches, I am not saying that people have license to believe anything no matter how absurd or ill-founded their beliefs happen to be. That would be ridiculous (and probably very good grounds for you to not bother finishing my book!). We should be able to give good reasons for why we believe something. However, the problem with the objection just mentioned is that it does not get to the heart of the matter. All that this objection can ever hope to demonstrate is perhaps how human beliefs about morality are formed rather than whether they are *true* or *false*.

In the interest of being intellectually honest, we must deal with the premises of an argument more directly if we want to refute them. Simply demonstrating how someone came to hold a belief, even if they came to hold such a belief in a sloppy and ham-fisted way, does not ultimately constitute a successful objection.

Even if we were to concede for the sake of argument that biological factors *do* play a role in how we form moral judgements, it does little to disprove the idea that "moral truths" are objective and truly exist. At most it would show that biological factors have helped us to *discover* moral values rather than invent them. It should be remembered that the theory of evolution is fundamentally a theory that seeks to explain the biodiversity of living things and ultimately does not provide answers as to whether God exists or not. So as it stands, we must conclude that this objection to the moral argument is not successful.

I tend to think that a few very radical atheists are inclined to introduce the concept of evolution into an argument due to its kind of "bogeyman" status among some Christians. For some atheists it is the ultimate "gotcha" objection and comeback. Some atheists may reason that if biological evolution was proven incontrovertibly true, then necessarily God need not, indeed cannot, exist. Since many assume that biological evolution is incontrovertibly true, they believe that by introducing this concept into any conversation about God they can ultimately short-circuit the whole affair with such a "knock-down" objection. Unfortunately, the logic simply does not follow here. Evolutionary theory simply does not have the tools in its toolbox to conclude that God does NOT exist. Another factor is that the belief in the God of Christianity and biological evolution are not *strictly* incompatible with one another.

There seem to be some good reasons for thinking that objective moral truths exist. Not only does every culture make a distinction between right and wrong, but our conscience tends to affirm to us (oftentimes very strongly) that some things are right and some things are wrong. Unless we are given very strong reasons for thinking our conscience is entirely off base in this matter, then I think we are well within our rights to trust that objective moral truths exist.

Perhaps the best reason to reject moral nihilism (and accept that objective moral truths really do exist), is that the consequences of moral nihilism are just too terrible to accept if another viable alternative is available. Indeed, this is why I think so many people who accept moral nihilism still live as if right and wrong really exist. The thought of a world where the actions of an Irena Sendler and a Heinrich Himmler are objectively no different is just too terrible to live with, so they often live inconsistently instead.

Why not consider the alternative that objective moral truths really do exist? Why not believe that love, compassion, and kindness are values that really exist, and that all people should strive to exemplify these values in their lives? If we can reasonably conclude that things like right and wrong really exist, then what explanation can we provide for their existence? Is it possible that God is the best explanation of their existence? Are you ready to jump into this next question?

# Chapter 5

# OBJECTIVE MORAL TRUTHS POINT TO THE EXISTENCE OF GOD

Have you ever begun the quest for deeper truth and realized that some of the alternatives to what you seek are far too terrifying to consider? While conducting my research, I gradually began to realize (rather strongly) that moral nihilism was too depressing and terrible a position to accept. Especially if a better alternative was available. The thought of a world in which the difference between hating someone and loving someone was objectively no different seemed unimaginably hopeless to me. I became convinced, and I remain convinced, that objective moral truths really *do* exist.

However, I still wondered if the existence of a transcendent moral lawgiver, namely God, was the best explanation for their existence. Distinguished thinkers such as Jerry Walls, David Baggett, William Lane Craig, C.S.

Lewis, and many others certainly thought so. Why was I still unsure?

Hours were spent in my little office wondering if I was giving into "wishful thinking." Is God really the best explanation for the existence of moral values? Was I simply trying to shoehorn this traditional and comforting belief into my life wherever I could? Prominent figures such as the American media mogul Ted Turner had compared religion to a "crutch" that "weak people" need to lean on in the difficult circumstances of life. As someone who has periodically struggled with low self-esteem, such comments stung and made me question my own strength and competence. Thus, I knew I needed to dig deeper. The moral argument intuitively made sense to me, but I needed to critically reflect on whether God was the best explanation for morality.

Indeed, other intelligent and articulate people, such as the prominent atheist Sam Harris, author of the bestselling book *The Moral Landscape,* argued that God is not necessary to establish and ground the existence of moral realities. Rather, science, logic, and reason can provide us with all the tools we need for building a moral and tranquil society. For Harris, atheism and objective moral truths are entirely compatible with one another.

With increased curiosity, I began to listen to what Sam Harris had to say and study his views more thoroughly. I watched him in various interviews and multiple formal debates with Christian thinkers and began to ask if there was in fact another explanation for objective moral truths other than a transcendent moral lawgiver: namely, God.

I was intrigued by the case Harris was making as he was quite ready to affirm that moral realities really exist. This was surprising to me as many other atheist thinkers I had read were either noncommittal about their existence or even openly rejected their existence.

As I began to study Harris's viewpoints more thoroughly, I discovered that he fits fairly comfortably (if not perfectly) within the paradigm of "Utilitarianism." Most historians of philosophy point to Jeremy Bentham as the founder of the philosophical system of "Utilitarianism." Bentham was an English jurist and philosopher who believed that the criteria for discerning between good and bad behaviors and actions was by assessing whether they produced the best results for the most people. For Bentham, if it could be determined that an action would produce the greatest amount of happiness for the greatest amount of people, then it was morally right. If an action failed to meet these standards, then it was deemed morally wrong by Bentham.

This theory brought to mind a story I once read. Though it may not be something you have read before, "The Lottery" by Shirley Jackson was a story that plays closely with such theories. The story is about a small town in New England. Each year a lottery takes place and everyone in town must participate. A family is chosen, and then a single family member. Once chosen, that family member is surrounded by everyone in town and is then stoned to death. This tradition seems to be for the good of the town. One death a year to keep the peace and happiness amongst the majority.

In his writings and lectures Harris has argued, similarly to Bentham, that morally right and wrong behaviors should be distinguished by whether they bring about the most good for the most people and contribute to human flourishing. Thinking back to "The Lottery," ask yourself this question: Could you stone someone to death if you knew that it was for the good of an entire town? Adding wood to the fire, Harris believes that science can determine what is best for the flourishing of humans, and that we can build a tolerant and peaceful society if we will simply follow the best insights of current scientific research.

Harris has become well known to many Westerners due to his scathing critiques of religion, particularly of the radical Islamic variety. Harris believes that religious belief has contributed greatly to human suffering due to its propensity to radicalize individuals. These radicalized individuals have in turn started multiple conflicts and committed horrific acts of terrorism due to their deeply held religious beliefs. Reflecting on this point, one cannot help but see, as with anything which becomes critically important to an individual, there is risk of creating the very thing we claim to fight against.

For Harris, religion is a blight upon human society because it has caused so much conflict, death, and division. He believes that it is high time for civilized and intelligent people to abandon primitive, superstitious, and counterproductive religious beliefs in favor of a society built on scientifically determined human values. Harris thinks that, on balance, religion has caused more harm to human society than good, and thus it should be abandoned by reasonable people. In his book *The Moral Landscape*, Harris makes this statement which provides important insight into his line of reasoning:

> Does forcing women and girls to wear burqas make a net positive contribution to human well-being? Does it produce happier boys and girls? Does it produce more compassionate men and more contented women? Does it make for better relationships between men and women, between boys and their mothers, or between girls and their fathers? I would bet my life that the answer to each of these questions is "no." So, I think, would many scientists.[4]

For Harris, the behaviors and practices he mentions are wrong because they do not better the human condition. Admittedly, some of Harris's critiques on religion are fair. Looking back through history, we can see times when religious movements have been repressive and detrimental to the cause of human well-being. With Harris, I denounce (in no uncertain terms) the evils of terrorism as well as the subjugation and abuse of women. Unfortunately, Harris paints with a very broad brush. He rushes to the judgement that all religious belief is false and unhelpful simply because *some* religious people throughout history have committed terrible atrocities.

In the interest of fairness, we can reasonably admit that some people have done very evil things due in large

---

4. Sam Harris, *The Moral Landscape: How Science Can Determine Human Values* (New York: Free Press, 2010), 65.

part to their deeply held religious beliefs. Despite the long list of terrible things that have happened throughout history stemming from religious extremism, it must also be recognized that many people have done very good things due to strongly held religious convictions. Indeed, the slave trade in the British Empire was outlawed in large part due to the efforts of Evangelical Christians. Many hospitals, universities, and relief organizations in existence today are the products of the Christian church. Mother Teresa was motivated to help the lepers of India largely because of her deeply held Christian convictions. When evaluating both sides of the coin, Harris's failure to recognize the great good that religion, and Christianity in particular, has done for the world seems a shortcoming of his worldview. Hardly the most problematic one he holds, as we shall soon see.

Followers of philosophical Utilitarianism (a group which I think Harris fits into reasonably well, if not perfectly) tend to take as a given that human beings have inherent value and thus the promotion of their well-being is good and praiseworthy. In *The Moral Landscape*, Harris frequently refers to and defends the concept of human well-being. On this point, Harris and I are in total agreement. All human beings deserve ethical treatment due to their inherent value. Expanding on this further, with Harris I would also affirm that because human beings are valuable, we should pursue policies that contribute to human well-being and flourishing.

Spring boarding off the basic concept that human beings indeed have inherent value, Harris's argument is then rather straightforward. Science has the requisite tools to help us determine what is best for human flourishing and well-being, and whatever is best for human flourishing can be considered a morally right thing to do. Whatever is detrimental to human flourishing can be considered a morally wrong thing to do. Based on his books and interviews, the general happiness of people and society is a major pillar of Harris's worldview. It is not surprising that his writings, thoughts, and worldview are attractive to many people. Not only does his approach to moral values seem to be reasonable, but it also takes the flourishing of human beings very seriously.

In my search for truth, I had to admit appreciation for Harris and his affirmation of moral values and the high priority he places on human flourishing (even if we would probably disagree on the details of what it means for human beings to flourish). However, despite this system's seeming positives and its rational attempt to provide a better explanation for the existence of objective moral truths than theism (belief in God's existence), during my research, I came to discover several important objections that can be levelled against Harris's thesis that I believe are successful.

As I stated earlier, Sam Harris places a very high value on human flourishing and happiness. For him, a society that produces the greatest amount of happiness for the greatest amount of people is simultaneously a just and praiseworthy one. While this idea seems reasonable enough, I don't think proponents of Harris's worldview have been able to adequately answer this objection: On what grounds can they say that a society with maximal human flourishing is better and morally superior to a society with maximal human misery?

I can hear the gears in your head spinning as you read this. Some of you are probably thinking that the question I have posed is absurd! "Isn't it just obviously true that a society filled with human flourishing is better than a society filled with human misery? Didn't you previously argue that experience and our own conscience strongly affirms for us that some things are right, and some things are wrong and that human beings have value?" These are reasonable questions, so bear with me a moment and I will elucidate.

Remember, Harris and I both agree that there are such things as objective moral truths. Both of us agree that things like terrorism and rape are objectively evil and deserve our strongest condemnation. On this point we have no disagreement. However, this is where our agreements end. We still have to answer this question: *What is the best explanation and foundation for objective moral truths?* Harris is an avowed atheist and critic of religion. Thus, while Harris argues mightily for the existence of moral values, what transcendent standard can he appeal to when he makes such moral judgements? When he affirms that people have value, what reason can he give for such an assertion? Indeed, I'm quite unsure that atheism can provide the necessary intellectual framework for such an assertion. And if human beings do not enjoy inherent value, how can we say that a world filled with human happiness is any better than a world filled with human suffering?

To answer this, I must speak from my place of faith. As someone who believes in God (and is a Christian more specifically), the standard I can appeal to when making moral judgements is God's inherent moral goodness. Any person who believes in God can reason similarly. If atheism is true, then what reason do I have for believing that people have value, and that human flourishing is preferable to human misery? It seems to me that if God exists, then it reasonably follows that people, whom he created, do have value. If atheism is true, then where does the value come from?

If we are simply the products of unguided evolution and our existence is merely an accident, on what grounds can anyone argue that human beings are indeed deserving of ethical treatment? Why do we have inherent dignity? In the evolutionary food chain, what reason can I claim for being any more valuable than an insect? Sure, I have greater cognitive and creative faculties than the insect, but these abilities are merely the result of a series of fortunate evolutionary accidents!

Whether I love my fellow humans or despise them is irrelevant. It will make little difference in the end. No judgement awaits me when I die. Why not live as selfishly as I desire? On atheism, all human actions and accomplishments will be proven meaningless when the universe reaches its inevitable heat death. Thus, while our conscience seems to affirm quite well the existence of objective moral truths, this same view mixes very poorly with atheism. If atheism is true, then we have little reason for thinking that these things really exist and that people have any inherent value. It seems in this equation, nothing and no one matters.

In my studying, it seemed Harris's perspective had a problem. Although he quite laudably affirms that objective moral truths really exist, his staunch atheism is a poor match with his belief in inherent human value. Now, to Harris's credit he does seem to recognize this important challenge to his worldview forthrightly and tries to give a good response to it. Indeed, he dubs this issue with his thesis the "value problem." Harris does attempt to solve the "value problem" in *The Moral Landscape* and demonstrate that moral values still very much exist even though God does not. Unfortunately for his worldview, I'm not confident his solution is successful.

You will recall that Harris defines something as morally good so long as it brings about the greatest amount of well-being for conscious creatures. While at first glance this may seem reasonable enough, all Harris has done is cleverly redefine what moral goodness is to make his thesis work. Unfortunately, simply engaging in the redefinition of terms will not solve the "value problem." The thoughts of eminent philosopher William Lane Craig are helpful in pointing out the weakness of Harris's argument:

> So, he [Harris] says, "Questions about values ... are really questions about the well-being of conscious creatures." Therefore, he concludes, "It makes no sense ... to ask whether maximizing well-being is 'good.'" Why not? Because he's redefined the word

"good" to *mean* the well-being of conscious creatures. So to ask, "Why is maximizing creatures' well-being good?" is on his definition the same as asking, "Why does maximizing creatures' well-being maximize creatures' well-being?" It is simply a tautology—talking in a circle. Thus, Harris has "solved" his problem simply by redefining his terms. It is mere word play.[5]

When I got right down to it, I felt there was a distinct and fundamental problem with Harris's thesis. While it has a lot to say about the flourishing of the human species, it still can't tell us why any of us have any right to flourish in the first place. Harris has not solved the "value problem" at all. He cannot tell us why a human has any more value than an insect or even why we should love and respect one another in an orderly society. On Harris's worldview I am not sure why someone would not be justified in pursuing their own "well-being" at the expense of others.

Harris forthrightly attempts to solve the "value problem," but his solution is less than satisfactory. Simply redefining terms will not do. However, searching for truth (the proverbial needle in a haystack), this is hardly the only problem I ran into with Harris's thesis. Truth be told, it may not even be its most problematic. Harris frequently

---

5. William Lane Craig, "Navigating Sam Harris' *The Moral Landscape*," Reasonable Faith, accessed June 24, 2019, https://www.reasonablefaith.org/writings/popular-writings/existence-nature-of-god/navigating-sam-harris-the-moral-landscape/.

states in his book how he is convinced that science can determine what human values ought to be. You will remember that Harris defines something as morally good if it brings the greatest amount of happiness to the most people, that is, if it meaningfully contributes to human flourishing.

For Harris, scientific research and common sense easily demonstrate that well-fed people are healthier than starving people and that people with access to Western standards of health care are healthier than those without it. Therefore, science and reason can determine what produces human well-being and that give us a moral framework to work with. Such a thesis seems reasonable and straightforward enough, but do science and reason really give us all the tools we need to discern the difference between right and wrong behavior?

I think an example may demonstrate why science and logic are probably not the magic wands that can solve all our difficulties when discerning the difference between what is right and what is wrong.

Picture this: You are walking through eighteenth-century China, somewhere in the countryside, when you come across two bandits who are mugging and attempting to rob another traveler. In their struggle to take your fellow traveler's money, they pull out knives and attempt to stab him without mercy.

Fortunately, you are able to fend off his attackers. Later, you tend his wounds so that he eventually recovers. Without your intervention, this man would have probably died. By providing for this man's well-being, you have done a morally right thing, or at least it would seem that way. However, what you do not know is that you have just saved the life of one of Mao-Se-Tung's ancestors. By saving this man's life, you have made possible the birth of one of the greatest mass murderers in history. Although by saving your fellow traveler's life you have provided for his well-being, you have also helped to bring about the incredible misery of millions of people.

Harris's worldview seemingly forces us to affirm some form of "consequentialism." Consequentialism is the view that we determine what is a right or wrong action based solely (or largely) on its consequences. The deeper that I got in my research, the more examples like the above showed me that consequentialism as a moral theory is fraught with difficulties.

While we may be able to marshal all the resources of our human faculties and science to determine with reasonable certainty what contributes to human well-being in the short-term, such tools, as powerful as they are, provide little success at determining long-term outcomes. An action that contributes to human well-being in the short-term may also set off a chain reaction of events that are ultimately disastrous for humanity. This stark reality suggests that consequentialism as a moral theory is problematic.

Science cannot predict the future with certainty and subsequently the ultimate consequences of our actions. It seems to me that if we must rely entirely, or even largely, on a consequentialist vision for morality (as it seems

Harris's thesis does) then we have little hope of forming confident moral judgements.

As a young pastor still committed to the existence of objective moral truths, I found that Harris's affirmation of moral values made his philosophy attractive, and I had to know more. Indeed, on the question of whether objective moral truths existed we were entirely in agreement. Indeed, while I reject Harris's firm commitment to atheism, his commitment to the existence of moral values is a very praiseworthy aspect of his moral theory. During my research he proved to be an intelligent and capable communicator of ideas. However, his worldview suffered from problems that I don't think he—or any other atheist—has offered satisfactory answers to. Harris cannot tell us why humans have inherent value and hence why they are deserving of ethical treatment. Nor can he tell us why a universe filled with maximal human flourishing is superior to one of maximal human misery.

If atheism is true, as Harris thinks it is, then we lack the tools we need to distinguish between right and wrong, good and bad, and the only thing larger than us is the universe itself in all its cold indifference. What pushed me forward to continue my research was more of the questions that remained unanswered. Harris failed to solve the "value problem" and resorts to an unhelpful tautology, and his moral vision requires us to affirm some form of "consequentialism," a system which in and of itself is probably not enough to determine what is right and what is wrong.

As I wrestled as a young pastor with the question of whether God existed, I began to realize the intellectual and emotional power of the "moral argument." You see, I understood intuitively and experientially, and I think most, if not all, people do as well, that there is a clear distinction between doing something that is cruel and doing something that is loving. As I held my little girl and sang "Jesus loves me" to her, I sensed deeply that this little child deserved to be nurtured and loved rather than neglected or abused. Any time I saw news reports of people being murdered by terrorists I sensed deeply that evil was at work. All of us have had similar experiences. Should we reject experiential evidence in favor of the existence of objective moral truths in exchange for the terrible difficulties of moral nihilism?

I am hardly the only person who has sensed deeply and intuitively that there is a clear difference between right and wrong. Virtually all people live as if objective moral truths exist and make moral judgements every day, even if they are ultimately unaware of it. The reality of such truths seemed so clear to me that I could not accept moral nihilism. And if they really do exist, and if we are going to be responsible thinkers, then we need to be able to provide a reasonable explanation for their existence. As I continued to study atheistic visions for the foundation of objective moral truths (such as Sam Harris's), they repeatedly came up short.

Some have suggested that we should simply accept moral truths as brute facts of human existence and leave it at that. However, it seems to me that a better explanation must surely be available. Shouldn't we want to know why human beings discern the difference between right and wrong and seek a reasonable explanation for it? Isn't a question as important as whether God exists or not worthy of our time? Slowly, painfully, and with plenty of doubts, I was beginning to understand that viewing God as the best explanation for the existence of objective moral truths intuitively made sense.

I began to realize that the existence of a transcendent moral lawgiver, namely God, was the best explanation for why all people groups have some sense of moral intuition as C.S. Lewis so wisely pointed out. Almost universally, people enjoy some sense of right and wrong because they are created by God. They are moral beings just as God is a moral being. If God exists, then we can responsibly say that there are certain moral standards that all people should live by. There is a transcendent standard of right and wrong that is binding upon us all. Rape, torture, and murder are wrong regardless of our present cultural circumstances.

The full range of human moral experience suggests very strongly that God exists.

Even though I had come to believe that the moral argument was powerful (and many professional philosophers and theologians agreed), my research would eventually reveal that this argument has periodically faced numerous objections over the centuries. Could the moral argument withstand careful scrutiny? Could these objections be answered? While I have already tried to respond to a handful of objections to the moral argument along the way, in the following chapter I will look at two of the most prominent contemporary objections to the moral argument. The search for truth continues...

## Chapter 6

# RESPONDING TO OBJECTIONS TO THE MORAL ARGUMENT

Debate after debate, I continued down the rabbit hole of information. I lost count as to how many I watched, but you can be sure that I learned a great deal about the moral argument by watching academic debates between atheists and Christians online. This doesn't discount the reading and research I was swimming in during this time, and in fact, many of the debates I found through my further research into the authors. After watching many of these debates, I noticed that atheists often objected to the moral argument by appealing to something they called the "Euthyphro Dilemma." Just what is this "dilemma" with such a funny name?

Although many have probably never heard of the Euthyphro Dilemma, its heritage goes all the way back to the Greek philosophers Socrates and Plato. David Baggett and Jerry Walls helpfully summarize how this dilemma came to be.

The Euthyphro Dilemma arises in an early dialogue of Socrates entitled, appropriately enough, *Euthyphro*. Written by his student Plato, the dialogue features Socrates questioning young Euthyphro about the true standard of morality. As a devout polytheist, Euthyphro attempts to explicate the nature and authority of morality in terms of the loves and hatreds of the gods. Since the Greek gods, by Euthyphro's own admission, could and likely did disagree about moral matters, Euthyphro is forced to say that morality is what all the gods agree on. If they all support a practice, it's an act of piety; if they all denounce a practice, it's an act of impiety.[6]

"That's all well and good, Julian, but just what does this heady little discussion between Euthyphro and Socrates about the Greek gods and morality have to do with the moral argument and God's existence?" I am so glad you asked.

Building on ideas presented in *Euthyphro*, contemporary atheist thinkers have repackaged aspects of Socrates and Euthyphro's dialogue. They suggested those who believe God is the best explanation for the existence of "objective moral truths" are faced with a real (and they would say *intractable*) dilemma. The Euthyphro Dilemma asks believers in God: *Are morally good actions good only because God commands us to do them (Euthyphro's answer)? Or does God command morally good actions because he is*

---

6. David Baggett and Jerry L. Walls, *Good God: The Theistic Foundations on Morality* (New York: Oxford University Pres, 2011), 32.

*bound to a higher standard of morality that ultimately does not originate with him?*

More simply put, the Euthyphro Dilemma states that "either something is good because God wills it, or else God wills something because it is good."[7]

As I continued searching for answers, this argument posed real problems for me, and certainly can create issues for believers in God. Particularly those who think that God is all powerful, morally perfect, and the author and originator of objective moral truths (as most Christians would).

As atheists pointed out in many of the debates I watched, both answers (whether we agree with Euthyphro or accept the alternative) create major theological difficulties for those who believe in God. They also seem to weaken the moral argument significantly. If we agree with Euthyphro and say that some actions are morally good simply because God commands them, and not because there is anything *objectively* good about them, then God would appear to be a somewhat arbitrary, even a morally ambiguous and mysterious, figure. Why is this so?

Critics of religious belief and the moral argument will sometimes say that if something is morally good *only* because God has commanded it, couldn't God just as easily command something entirely *different*? While it seems reasonable, perhaps even self-evident, to say that God

---

7. William Lane Craig, *Reasonable Faith: Christian Truth and Apologetics* (Wheaton, IL: Crossway, 2008), 181.

wants us to love one another, couldn't he just as easily command us to *hate* one another? Would stealing from someone be right if God commanded it? Could God arbitrarily change his mind about what is right and wrong and condemn murder one day and condone it the next?

If we agree with Euthyphro, then God's character seems impossible to know and if his approach to morality is entirely arbitrary, is God someone whom we can really trust? A God who is morally ambiguous and entirely arbitrary in his moral commands cannot be reconciled with the benevolent and loving God that most Christians believe in.

What if we reject Euthyphro's answer and accept the alternative? Are we in a better place? Is the moral argument made secure once more? Probably not. If we accept the alternative and say that God is bound to a standard of morality that did not originate with him then it is far from clear that the existence of objective moral truths would point to God's existence.

How can God be the transcendent moral lawgiver if morality doesn't originate with God? If we disagree with Euthyphro and accept the alternative, then one of the premises of the moral argument—namely, that God is the best explanation for the existence of objective moral truths (because he is ultimately the source of them)—is severely weakened or even undone.

If God is not the author of morality and is bound to a moral standard independent of himself, then God starts to look less and less like the God that most Christians believe in and looks more like the finite and petty gods of the Greek pantheon. If God is not the transcendent moral lawgiver, the author and source of morality, then does he have any right to tell us how to live?

Discovering the moral argument while still in the throes of my crisis of faith made me feel as if someone had thrown my faith a much-needed life preserver. However, whenever atheists shared tricky rebuttals to the moral argument (such as the Euthyphro Dilemma) my newfound confidence would waver. The moral argument intuitively made sense to me, but hearing intelligent and persuasive atheist voices such as Sam Harris and Richard Dawkins critique it made me doubt all over again. During this quest for truth, I would sit in my little office and wonder whether it was even worth it. Maybe I should quit the quest, quit the ministry, and retry my talents at being a professional musician again. Perhaps enough long nights playing music in coffeehouses would help me push these tricky intellectual questions out of my mind.

My friend Bill from college once told me, "It's impossible to know what moral truth is; there are simply too many moral codes to choose from." That statement combined with the Euthyphro Dilemma made the problem seem even more intractable. As far as Bill was concerned, we should pursue whatever makes us happy and forget about the sort of difficult kinds of questions I was asking Fixing up old cars made Bill happy, and music made me happy. Maybe I should follow his example?

It sounded all well and good in my head; however, I knew I could not live that way. I had to see whether the Euthyphro Dilemma could be solved. Even if I ran from my quest and from the ministry, I knew my questions would relentlessly follow me. The only solution was to pursue the truth at all costs. The quest had to continue.

The Euthyphro Dilemma seemed to present real problems for the moral argument, and it certainly challenged my already shaken faith. I could see how many atheist thinkers believed it to be a devastating objection to the moral argument and thus are fond of bringing it up in academic debates and informal discussions. However, is it possible that the Euthyphro Dilemma is really a false dilemma upon closer examination? Philosophers Jerry Walls and David Baggett suggest in *Good God: The Theistic Foundations of Morality* that a third option is available to us, and the Euthyphro Dilemma is not insurmountable.[8]

According to Walls and Baggett, rather than saying that something is good simply because God commands it or that God merely conforms to a higher standard of goodness that is ultimately independent of him, we ought to say that not only is the "ultimate good" dependent upon God, but "God *just is* the ultimate Good."[9] Let's unpack and explore this line of reasoning a little more. If we embrace either option of Euthyphro's Dilemma, problems inevitably result. However, if we say that God is the ultimate good and that objective moral truths are grounded

8. Baggett and Walls, *Good God: The Theistic Foundations on Morality*, 86-87.

9. Ibid., 92, 130.

in his perfectly good nature, then the problems presented by the Euthyphro Dilemma disappear.

If God is the ultimate good and moral truths are grounded in his nature, then his commands will be anything but arbitrary. God is not bound to a moral standard independent of himself. He is bound only to the constraints of his nature. Fortunately, by nature God is good, loving, compassionate, righteous, and just. Thus, on this line of reasoning, we need not fear a world where God is a mysterious, morally ambiguous, and arbitrary figure. A God who could on a whim condemn murder one day and condone it the next. With Christian philosophers like Walls, Baggett, and William Lane Craig we should affirm that "all of God's commands are deeply resonant with his character" and by nature God is good, loving, and kind.[10] Such a God will never command evil. Indeed "a being in whom the whole moral law resides could hardly fail to be perfectly good."[11]

During my spiritual and intellectual journey, I frequently encountered the Euthyphro Dilemma, most often while watching academic debates about the existence of God online or when reading books about the moral argument. Sometimes, I would see it mentioned in online discussion forums. While I knew I needed to study the Euthyphro Dilemma to have a thorough understanding of the moral argument, I must confess that the Euthyphro,

---

10. Ibid., 126.
11. Ibid., 51.

while challenging on an *intellectual* level, did not resonate with me nearly as much on an *emotional* level. "What do you mean, Julian?"

Doubts about Jesus's resurrection, questions about what happens after we die, paying bills, antibiotic resistance, saving enough money for retirement (you get the point)—these things kept me up at night (and sometimes still do) and caused me a great deal of anxiety. The Euthyphro Dilemma, not so much. The "problem of evil" objection to the moral argument proved to be both *intellectually* and *emotionally* challenging to me. Indeed, even the eminent philosopher, theologian, and Christian apologist William Lane Craig has called the problem of evil "the greatest obstacle to belief in the existence of God."[12] Stated very simply, the problem of evil asks, "If an all-powerful and morally perfect God really exists, then why is there so much evil in the world?"

For the atheist, the problem of evil presents a powerful defeater for the moral argument and God's existence. They will frequently argue that the existence of so much evil in the world suggests that God is either unconcerned with human suffering and therefore not morally perfect, or that God is too weak to do anything about the world's evil and is therefore not all powerful. Many atheists are convinced that if the problem of evil objection is success-

---

12. William Lane Craig, "The Problem of Evil," Reasonable Faith, accessed September 19, 2022, https://www.reasonablefaith.org/writings/popular-writings/existence-nature-of-god/the-problem-of-evil/.

ful, then God's existence is significantly less likely. In fact, so much less likely, that atheism would be far more reasonable than belief in God.

Are you a deeply empathetic person? For me, I have always been a deeply sensitive person who feels quite acutely the pain and suffering of others. Perhaps it is one of the reasons I chose to be a pastor. I always hoped I might alleviate the suffering of people and give them hope. Even before I encountered the so-called problem of evil in the scholarly literature, I felt this objection's force in my everyday life. Remember when I shared about seeing the attacks on the World Trade Center in 2001? Even as a child, I wept for the victimized and was utterly perplexed by the hatred of those who were willing to sacrifice their lives in order to kill countless others. As a pastor, I have counseled people who have lost very small children, who have been stolen from, or who have been sexually abused by people they trusted. It isn't a secret that we live in a world where terrorism, human trafficking, and conflict are ever-present and seemingly inescapable realities. Even as a Christian pastor, and especially during this journey searching for truth, I have sometimes asked God in desperation, "Where are you?"

Although the problem of evil never proved fatal to my faith (even during my spiritual and intellectual struggles), this has not always been the case for other people. Indeed, the renowned New Testament scholar Bart Ehrman, a former Evangelical Christian who now claims to be an agnostic, has noted that he rejected Christianity in part because of the problem of evil. Does the problem of evil ultimately defeat the moral argument? Does it render belief in God unreasonable? Based on my research and study, I don't think so. In fact, I have come to believe that Christianity has all the resources it needs to adequately answer the problem of evil.

Most philosophers tend to make a distinction between the "intellectual" problem of evil and the "emotional" problem of evil. According to William Lane Craig, "The intellectual problem of evil concerns how to give a rational explanation of how God and evil can co-exist. The emotional problem of evil concerns how to dissolve people's emotional dislike of a God who would permit suffering."[13]

If we want to provide a thorough response to the problem of evil, then we must adopt an approach that can answer both the intellectual and emotional sides of the problem. Let's tackle the *intellectual* side of the problem first.

From my experience, very few atheists will insist that it is logically *impossible* for God and evil to coexist.[14] However, they will often say that the sheer magnitude of evil that exists in our world suggests very strongly that there is no God. Or if there is a God, he is a weak God who is too impotent to do anything to extinguish the forces of evil in the world. This picture of God is hardly

---

13. Craig, "The Problem of Evil," https://www.reasonablefaith.org/writings/popular-writings/existence-nature-of-god/the-problem-of-evil/.
14. Ibid.

consistent with the God that most Christians (or probably even most Theists) believe in.

How are we to adequately respond to the intellectual problem of evil? In my research I have found two responses to be quite helpful.

Eminent philosophers Jerry Walls and David Baggett,
as well as the Anglican churchman A.C. Ewing, share
that ultimately God is not to blame for the problem of
evil, rather, the human abuse of free will is.[15] Historically
speaking, most Christian theologians have affirmed that
just as God is a being with free will, human beings enjoy
free will as well. That is, human beings are *genuinely* free
to choose good or evil. Because of this, human beings can
either choose to conform to the objective moral truths
that God has revealed to us or reject them and conform to
our own moral standards which are often highly deficient
and sometimes even evil.

Some may counter by arguing that if the human abuse
of free will has caused so much suffering and evil, then
why did God give human beings free will in the first
place? Is free will a blessing or a curse? Is it an utterly
misguided idea on God's part? Amid my faith crisis, I had
no answers to these questions. Looking back now, I would
say that God has created human beings with free will because God so strongly values the possibility of having *genuine* and loving relationships with us. For genuine, loving

---

15. Baggett and Walls, *Good God: The Theistic Foundations on Morality*,
151-153.

relationship to exist between God and human beings, free will must exist as well. Love is something that must be freely given and freely received. God understands this truth even better than we do.

If God created us in such a way that we could only choose him and the good, that the option to reject him and turn to evil was not actually possible, then it would not be a genuine, loving relationship. If this were the case, human beings would be more like sophisticated computer programs created by a skilled software engineer. While a computer program can complete meaningful tasks and even bring a certain kind of delight to its programmer, it would be far-fetched to say the programmer has a *relationship* with the program he or she created.

While free will necessarily entails the possibility that human beings will abuse it and do great evil, God has given human beings free will because genuine, loving relationships are so important, so essential to a truly meaningful life. Almost all people, regardless of their religious beliefs, can appreciate the wonder and beauty of friendship, collegiality, community, and romance, that is, genuine, loving relationship. Thus, while free will is a double-edged sword in that human beings can use it for good or ill, it is entirely necessary if we want to live in a world where genuine, loving relationships are a real possibility.

"But why doesn't God intervene more in our world to stop the forces of evil? Is he powerless to do anything about evil or does he simply not care?" Answering the question of why God permits suffering in this world is a challenging one. Nevertheless, I think Christian philosophers and theologians have offered some good responses to this difficult question.

Perhaps the strongest response I have found in my research to this difficult query would be that God in his wisdom has morally sufficient reasons for allowing evil to exist in our world. Is it possible that God can permit evil actions that will later contribute to the greater good? As human beings with limited intelligence and an uncertain knowledge of the future and how it interacts with the past, we may not be able to immediately see how God will permit evil to someday contribute to the greater good. Just because we can't see it or even envision it, does not mean God cannot work in this way. Especially if God has exhaustive foreknowledge of future events as most Christians believe.

Eminent philosopher, theologian, and Christian apologist William Lane Craig puts it this way.

> As finite persons, we are limited in time, space, intelligence, and insight. But the transcendent and sovereign God sees the end from the beginning and providentially orders history so that His purposes are ultimately achieved through human free decisions. In order to achieve His ends, God may have to put up with certain evils along the way. Evils which appear pointless to us within our limited framework may be seen to have been justly permitted within God's wider framework.[16]

---

16. Craig, "The Problem of Evil," https://www.reasonablefaith.org/writings/popular-writings/existence-nature-of-god/the-problem-of-evil/.

Now, someone might reasonably ask, "All of this sounds fine and dandy in theory, but can we actually produce any examples of how evil later contributed to the greater good?" I could tell you many different historical instances that show how God's larger framework has affected the world, but perhaps if we look closer to how each of us could be affected, you can better see what I mean.

## THE BOAT ACCIDENT

On a sunny day in a small town in California, tragedy struck. Lewis, an avid boater, had asked his dad if he and a friend could take the boat out for a bit. His dad of course said yes. Despite being just 16, Lewis was talented and was more than capable of being safe on the water. No one knows what happened, but Lewis fell off the boat, hitting his head and despite valiant efforts on behalf of the local emergency crews, Lewis perished.

There is no bigger hurt for a parent than the loss of a child. No Band-Aid we can offer, and words often offer little help to a grieving family. After his passing, during the funeral, hundreds of children decided to follow Jesus, largely because of Lewis's vibrant faith and love for others. A year later, his parents, not yet ready to be empty nesters, decided to adopt. What happened next is nothing short of a miracle. They found two girls, sisters, one who was nearly about to age out of adoption at 16 years old. In their country, when you age out of adoption you end up homeless, on the street, and that sadly left many girls with few options. Many resorted to prostitution to survive.

Of the two sisters, the younger sister (13) had previously had the opportunity to be adopted but had refused because she didn't want to be separated from her sister. Now, adopted by Lewis's parents, these two girls were brought to the US to become part of a fractured and hurting family. The result was healing and hope. Nothing would replace Lewis. He is still mourned daily. Yet within the despair of loss, there is hope. Had Lewis not died, those hundreds of lives may never have fully realized who their Savior is. Had Lewis not died, those girls may have ended up on the street or worse, trapped in a life of poverty and abuse.

The evils and travesties of our lives do serve a greater purpose. We may not see it when we are mired in the pain of it. Watching the suffering of others while it seems that no one, not even God, cares anymore. Instead, there is a tapestry of good waiting for us that will be revealed in due time. That doesn't mean the evils of this world don't hurt us. It means that they serve a greater purpose we may not be able to see right now.

When the Christian is faced with the challenging problem of evil, they can respond that while our world is indeed plagued by evil, because there is a God, it need not be irredeemable evil. Not only can God permit evil so as to bring about the greater good, but Christian theology teaches that one day God will provide ultimate justice to all the world's victimized.

If atheism is true, then it seems that the problem of evil is made much worse. Without God, we may very well live in a world with a great deal of irredeemable evil. Where millions of people's suffering is ultimately meaningless, where the victimized will never receive justice, where there is no hope of an afterlife for those whose lives were cut mercilessly short. Looked at this way, the problem of evil may actually point us toward God rather than away from God, for who else us can plausibly save us from our terrible predicament?

Now that I have attempted to address the intellectual problem of evil, the emotional problem of evil remains. While someone who is struggling with the intellectual problem of evil will struggle to see how God and evil can logically coexist, the person who is struggling with the emotional problem of evil will express frustration, even dislike, toward God because they perceive he does not do enough to alleviate evil and human suffering in the world.

For the person struggling with the emotional problem of evil, the responses I have just provided to the intellectual problem of evil may seem cold, callous, and unhelpful. Furthermore, as someone with a pastor's heart I have come to discover (with a great deal of help from my wife Allison) that when someone is hurting, and they are wondering why God would allow their hurt, they typically don't need heady and philosophical answers to their questions. They need support, community, and love. They need an ear that is ready to listen. They need pastoral and sensitive answers to difficult questions.

People who struggle with the emotional problem of evil often wonder if God really cares about their suffering. Or is God really just the cold and distant God of the Deists, the "clockmaker" God, who got humanity and the universe off to a fine start but has mostly left us to our own devices.

Well, if Christianity is true, then God is not cold and distant. Rather, God is loving, compassionate, and intimately concerned with human suffering. This reality is clearly proven in the life and ministry of Jesus Christ. Indeed, Jesus was willing to endure all the hardships associated with the human condition and even be brutally murdered on a cross to show us God's love. The eminent and much celebrated philosopher Alvin Plantinga puts it beautifully:

> As the Christian sees things, God does not stand idly by, coolly observing the suffering of His creatures. He enters into and shares our suffering. He endures the anguish of seeing his son, the second person of the Trinity, consigned to the bitterly cruel and shameful death of the cross. Christ was prepared to endure the agonies of hell itself . . . in order to overcome sin, and death, and the evils that afflict our world, and to confer on us a life more glorious that we can imagine. He was prepared to suffer on our behalf, to accept suffering of which we can form no conception.[17]

To the person suffering from the emotional problem of evil, traditional Christian theology teaches that God cares deeply for human beings and resonates deeply with

---

17. Alvin Plantinga, "Self-Profile," in *Alvin Plantinga*, ed. James E. Tomberlin and Peter van Inwagen, Profile 5 (Dordrecht: D. Reidel, 1985), 36.

our hurts and struggles. So much so, that God was willing to endure our hardships and struggles with us in the person of Jesus of Nazareth. The God of Christianity has not turned his back on the suffering of humanity, he endured alongside of us.

This treasure hunt for truth was helping me make real progress on my spiritual and intellectual journey. After a period of serious doubt about God's existence, confidence in my faith was gradually returning because reason, evidence, and experience attested to me that there was a God. Although I was (and still am) impressed with the moral argument and even the emotional and intelligent discussions on the existence of evil, all it did for me was suggest strongly that God exists. It still left me with the question of whether Christianity was true. Indeed, many people who believe in God could affirm some form of the moral argument. How was I to know that Christianity was true and not one of the world's other great religions?

The moral argument was my dead end in this query. I realized my intellectual and spiritual quest was only beginning. Though I was now confident that God existed, I needed to know if he had revealed himself to humanity in any clear and decisive way. I knew intellectually why I believed in God, but I was still struggling to articulate reasons for why I should be a Christian.

Truthfully, this may have been the most painful part of my intellectual journey. I never doubted the existence of God as much as I doubted the unique claims of the Christian faith. I considered whether Islam was true and nearly abandoned the Christian faith several times. There were days that I was such an emotional wreck with no stable foot of truth to place my trust on that I could barely eat (a remarkable feat for me!), sleep, or work. Many of the activities that I had previously enjoyed no longer interested me. I can remember many a Saturday night spent in my easy chair not able to shake the question of whether Christianity was true or if I had grown up living a lie. Was the Bible study or sermon I was about to deliver the following day true? Could I know with confidence that God has revealed himself to us? The journey for the truth was picking up speed and I was about to discover something that was going to change my world.

# Chapter 7

# WHAT CAN WE KNOW ABOUT JESUS?

"Am I right back where I started?"

That was the question that was on my mind in the fall of 2014. I was increasingly confident that God existed. My research into the moral argument demonstrated that it was persuasive enough to warrant my belief in God, or a higher power. One who had instilled in us some sense of moral values and duties. Despite this knowledge, I still doubted whether Christianity was true.

If someone were to ask me why I was a Christian, could I give them a good answer? I could share with them how I accepted Christ as Savior and Lord at summer camp and how I powerfully experienced the love, mercy, and forgiveness of God (an experience that I by no means wish to invalidate, nor ever could!). However, could I share with them why they should be a Christian too? Could I give them reasons for believing that Christianity was the worldview that best corresponded to reality?

The answer to these questions evaded me, and my inability to answer them ate away at me almost continually. As such, I found many of my pastoral duties that I had previously enjoyed just dreadful. I felt like a hypocrite every time I preached. Sometimes I had little desire to teach the Christian faith to the students entrusted to my spiritual care. Whenever I led Christians in the singing of hymns, I wondered if the Savior (Jesus of Nazareth) we were singing to was really listening. I was reasonably confident that there was a God, and this assured me that I, and the people I loved, had value. That much felt pretty certain to me. Yet, unless I could articulate better reasons to believe that Christianity was true, I knew my faith would remain anemic. Thus, my research had to continue. I needed to learn whether there was a good way or not to verify the truth claims of the Christian faith.

The studies continued. My research began anew by investigating whether the biblical record was historically reliable and accurate. In those days, I reasoned that if I could prove that the Bible contained no errors, then the truthfulness of my faith would seemingly be confirmed. I read books by biblical scholars from many different backgrounds. Some of these scholars were committed Christians who thought there were good reasons to think the Bible was historically reliable.

However, truth isn't always found in an echo chamber. To keep with my theme of seeking truth in all places, I also read books by skeptical biblical scholars who thought the very opposite. I read several books by the skeptical New Testament scholar Bart Ehrman, who was at one time a devout Evangelical Christian but now claims to be an agnostic. During this time, I read his book *Jesus, Interrupted* and I was shocked by what I found in its pages! At that time, I thought that Ehrman made a powerful case that the New Testament could not be trusted and was historically unreliable. My opinion of this book has changed considerably with time, but when I first read it, it made quite an impression on me. Ehrman's writings did nothing to strengthen my faith.

As I continued to read, I found a book that interested me largely due to its engaging title. It was called *Seeking Allah, Finding Jesus* by Nabeel Qureshi. I found the title intriguing since I was questioning my own faith and I was actively researching Islam to see whether it was true. Much of the book was Qureshi's spiritual autobiography. He shared in detail how he was raised in a devout Muslim family but later converted to Christianity. In his book he talked of how several intelligent and caring Christians took him under their wing and shared with him the evidence for the resurrection of Jesus. In his book, Qureshi candidly admitted that even while he was still a devout Muslim, he thought that the historical evidence for the resurrection of Jesus was impressive. I reasoned that if the historical evidence for the resurrection was strong enough to impress a devout Muslim, I needed to investigate this line of evidence thoroughly.

Qureshi's book was quite helpful, even paradigm-shifting, in terms of how it shaped my thinking on the best way to verify the truth claims of the Christian faith. In *Seeking Allah, Finding Jesus*, Nabeel did argue in favor of the historical reliability of the Bible. However, he wrote a great deal more about how the historical evidence for the resurrection of Jesus convinced him that Christianity was true.

This journey taught me that although it is important to study the Bible's historical reliability, what matters most is that Jesus is who he says he is, and that God indeed placed his stamp of approval on him by raising him from the dead after his crucifixion. Christianity could be shown to be true and reasonable even if I could never prove that absolutely everything the Bible says is true.

Through reading Qureshi's work, I realized that *Jesus* is the *foundation* and *cornerstone* of the Christian faith and if we confirm that his resurrection enjoys historical support then Christianity's truthfulness would be confirmed. Indeed, the Apostle Paul, one of early Christianity's most important figures, affirmed that the truth of the Christian faith rises and falls on whether the resurrection of Jesus really happened (See 1 Corinthians 15 in the Christian Bible). If we want to know whether Christianity is true, we *must* investigate the resurrection of Jesus.

Thus, my research into whether the resurrection of Jesus could be historically verified had begun. I was already convinced that there was a God, so belief in the supernatural, even the miraculous, was not out of bounds. If there is a God, then miracles are at least a possibility that we need to consider. Could it be possible that God had revealed himself powerfully to us by resurrecting Jesus from the dead?

You can imagine that as I began my research on the resurrection of Jesus, I came up against objections to its truth very quickly. One objection that surprised me, and even took me a little off guard, was that the resurrection of Jesus could not have happened simply because Jesus was not a historical person in the first place. Well-known authors such as Richard Carrier and Robert M. Price were making this case and many atheists who were active online frequently quoted their work. This objection surprised me because even highly skeptical scholars like Bart Ehrman had never gone this far in any of their books. Still, based on what I knew at the time, I had to wrestle with this objection. Could we know anything about Jesus? Was he a historical, flesh-and-blood person?

A fundamental rule of historical research is that to write good and accurate history, consultation of numerous independent and reliable primary sources is indispensable. Primary sources will date to or around the time of the person or event in question and contain firsthand accounts and eyewitness testimony. In general, historians believe that when two independent primary sources agree on an event's reality, the credibility of both sources are substantially increased.[18] Finally, if two sources agree about a historical event, then that event's reality becomes significantly more plausible. These foundational princi-

---

18. Martha Howell and Walter Prevenier, *From Reliable Sources: An Introduction to Historical Methods* (Ithaca: Cornell University Press, 2001), 69-87.

ples of historical research will guide our discussion going forward.

Do we have any good historical sources about Jesus's life?

While conducting my research, I discovered that we do in fact have numerous and credible historical sources about Jesus's life. The ancient Roman historian and senator Tacitus, writing around 116 CE in his famous Annals, mentions Jesus of Nazareth and his early followers when commenting on the great fire that destroyed much of Rome during Nero's day.

Tacitus states:

> Nero fastened the guilt and inflicted the most exquisite tortures on a class hated for their abominations, called Christians by the populace. Christus, from whom the name had its origin, suffered the extreme penalty during the reign of Tiberius at the hands of one of our procurators, Pontius Pilatus, and a most mischievous superstition, thus checked for the moment, again broke out not only in Judæa, the first source of the evil, but even in Rome, where all things hideous and shameful from every part of the world find their centre and become popular.[19]

In this document, written close to the lifetime of Jesus (if Jesus was crucified sometime around 33 CE then this would only be about 80 years after his lifetime, which is very good by ancient standards), we find a couple of important affirmations about "Christus." Most scholars are

---

19. Tacitus, *Annals* 15.44.

convinced that the so-called "Christus" in this account is probably a reference to Jesus of Nazareth (the name "Christus" probably being a derivative of the Greek word "Christos" which means Messiah and one of the earliest titles ascribed to Jesus). Not only do we find an affirmation of Jesus's existence, but we also are told that he was executed by Pontius Pilate and that during his lifetime he amassed a following that apparently had grown and spread to Rome by the time of the great fire (about 64 CE).

This source is very important as Tacitus is typically thought by many modern historians to be a sober and careful historian. His testimony to the existence and life of Jesus gives us some grounds for believing that Jesus existed historically. However, Tacitus is hardly the only source that attests to Jesus's existence, as I was about to find out.

Perhaps you are familiar with the Jewish historian Josephus. As a child I had heard pastors mention him in sermons, but I had never bothered to read his work myself. It would only be at this point in my life that I would learn about his significance. One of Josephus's best-known works is his *Antiquities of the Jews,* written sometime around 93-94 CE. In this record of Jewish history, Josephus mentions Jesus in two places. Once he mentions Jesus only briefly noting that "Jesus … was called the Christ."[20] However, in another section of Josephus's

---

20. Josephus, *Antiquities*, 20.9.1.

*Antiquities* he speaks about Jesus in much more detail. Josephus says:

> Now there was about this time Jesus, a wise man, if it be lawful to call him a man; for he was a doer of wonderful works, a teacher of such men as receive the truth with pleasure. He drew over to him both many of the Jews and many of the Gentiles. He was [the] Christ. And when Pilate, at the suggestion of the principal men amongst us, had condemned him to the cross, those that loved him at the first did not forsake him; for he appeared to them alive again the third day; as the divine prophets had foretold these and ten thousand other wonderful things concerning him. And the tribe of Christians, so named from him, are not extinct at this day.[21]

Now, let me say now that numerous experts have many reservations about the passage just cited (sometimes called the "Testimonium Flavianum" by scholars). First, in this passage it states, in no uncertain terms, that Jesus was "The Christ" while in the much shorter passage quoted earlier that he was simply "called Christ." The fact that the longer passage suggests that Jesus was divine (recall, "if it be lawful to call him a man"), was a wise man, a great teacher, and that he experienced resurrection after his crucifixion seems very uncharacteristic of Josephus who was probably not a Christian. Because of these difficulties, many scholars have wondered what to do with this longer passage in Josephus's *Antiquities*. If the scholars had

21. Ibid, 18.3.3

questions about this longer passage in *Antiquities*, could I have any confidence in any of the writings of Josephus as historical sources for the life of Jesus?

Surprisingly, for me at least, the answer of many respected historians of antiquity was yes! First, almost every historian of antiquity accepts the shorter passage as being a good source to authenticate the existence of Jesus of Nazareth. The source is a good one because it was written shortly after Jesus's purported lifetime, shows little sign of exaggeration or embellishment and many historians of antiquity think that Josephus was a reasonably sober historian who was genuinely concerned with writing accurate history. Although the shorter passage from *Antiquities* does not give us a great deal of information about Jesus, about all it can confirm is that he existed and that he was called "Christ," it remains a good source for the life of Jesus.

Second, I also learned (again to my surprise) that many historians of antiquity thought that the longer passage in *Antiquities* was a useful source for the life of Jesus as well. While most are convinced that somewhere along the way an enterprising Christian author added portions (most notably the references to Jesus being divine and experiencing resurrection) to Josephus's larger passage, they also think that several important parts of the passage are authentic and that it serves as a good source for the life of Jesus.[22]

---

22. Michael R. Licona, *The Resurrection of Jesus: A New Historiographical Approach* (Downers Grove, IL: IVP Academic, 2010), 235-242.

Although the passage in its original form is now lost to us, historians are convinced that the original would have probably affirmed that Jesus existed, was crucified by Pontius Pilate, was a teacher who amassed a following, and that some people in Josephus's day still respected and remembered Jesus's teachings.

Now that I knew we had multiple helpful sources such as Tacitus and Josephus to confirm a few of the most basic details about Jesus's life, my attention turned to the Gospels of Matthew, Mark, Luke, and John that we find in the New Testament. Although the sources of Tacitus and Josephus confirmed Jesus's existence and ministry, I was now asking deeper questions about Jesus such as *How did Jesus understand himself? Did he consider himself divine? Did he understand himself as being God's unique representative to humankind?*

I knew I needed to explore these questions thoroughly in my journey toward truth as mainstream Christianity affirms far more than Jesus's mere existence. Historically, most Christians have believed that Jesus understood himself as divine and have worshipped him as God in the flesh. I knew that if my quest for truth was to reach a successful conclusion, I needed to see if there was any warrant to these beliefs. Knowing a few very basic details about Jesus's life might be sufficient for the historically curious, but for someone still wondering whether I could confidently place my faith in Jesus, this was not enough. I had to know if what I had traditionally believed about Jesus was true. My quest had to go on, despite how weary and discouraged I often was.

If I wanted to know more than just a few basic details about Jesus's life, if I wanted to "paint" an accurate portrait of who the Jesus of history was, I would have to wrestle with the question of whether the Gospels, ostensibly sober biographies of Jesus of Nazareth, were useful historical sources for Jesus's life in the same way that Josephus and Tacitus's writings were.

Now, some readers may object to my appealing to the Gospels to support the case for Jesus's resurrection. Indeed, when discussing this issue with skeptics I have heard things like, "You can't appeal to Christianity's sacred text to demonstrate its truthfulness; that's reasoning in a circle." My response to this line of reasoning would be this: In building my case for the resurrection I will not appeal to the Gospels as *divine revelation* (even though as a committed Christian I do believe the Gospels to be divinely inspired). Nor will I try to argue that we can trust the Gospels on historical matters because they contain no errors (even though as a theologian I am comfortable affirming the Bible's infallibility).

Rather, in this book I will appeal to the Gospels only as useful and reliable *historical sources* for the life of Jesus. Indeed, the Gospels are our earliest (and best) historical sources for the life of Jesus and to ignore them when studying his life would be historiographical malpractice.[23] I will in short order show how multiple professional New Testament scholars and historians of antiquity are con-

---

23. Licona, 207.

vinced that the Gospels can be mined for useful historical knowledge.

Beginning an extensive study on the historical value of the Gospels brought back for me earlier memories of studying at a state university. Studying at a university with students from many different backgrounds opened many doors for discussions about religious belief. I recalled a discussion I had with someone during my freshman year in college about the Bible and its historical reliability. After sharing with her that the Bible was essential to my faith, she began to share a little about her religious background. She related that although she had been raised as a Christian, she had begun to question her faith in her teen years mainly due to misgivings about the Bible.

She explained that we could know very little about Jesus of Nazareth since the Gospels were not written until hundreds of years after his lifetime. During this period between his lifetime and the composition of the Gospels, legends accrued around the person of Jesus. Thus, by the time the Gospels were written their authors could no longer separate fact from fiction about Jesus. Because of this, the Gospels contained many stories about Jesus that had never taken place in history.

Since the Gospels were riddled with legendary material, we could not separate what was fact from fiction in them and we could know very little about who Jesus really was. For her, the Gospels contained some value in terms of the ethics and morals that they taught, but they had little historical value. I did not know how to respond to her. At that time, I knew little about the history of the Gospels.

Remarkably, now that I was beginning an extensive study on the Gospels, I was about to find out that almost everything she believed about the Gospels was *wrong*!

Many people believe that the Gospels were written hundreds of years after Jesus's earthly lifetime and that they are of little historical value. However, most professional scholars of the New Testament are convinced that this is not the case. In fact, most scholars believe that the Gospel of Mark was written sometime around 60 CE, Matthew and Luke around 70 CE, and John sometime around 90 CE. If Jesus completed his earthly ministry sometime around 33 CE then this means that Mark was written only about 25 years or so after Jesus's earthly ministry and the other Gospels were written between 30 to 60 years after his ministry.

This is significant as all the Gospels were written within a time frame sufficiently close to Jesus's lifetime that eyewitnesses to his life and ministry would have still been alive during their composition. They could have contributed valuable information to these works and presumably offered corrections when needed. The fact that the Gospels were written rather close to Jesus's lifetime greatly increases their usefulness as historical sources.

If you find yourself unimpressed with these facts that are generally agreed upon by most professional New Testament scholars and many historians of antiquity, I ask you to pause and consider this: The earliest biography we have of Alexander the Great, written by the great historian Plutarch, was written nearly 300 years after Alexander's lifetime and yet many professional scholars of antiquity think it to be a basically historically reliable biography. Do we have any reason to be more skeptical of the Gospels when we consider how closely they were written to their subject's lifetime? Especially when they are compared to other biographies of antiquity.

Historically speaking, we are in a much better situation about Jesus than with many other ancient figures. Not only do we have the sources of Josephus and Tacitus which can give us a few very basic details about Jesus's life, but we also have four biographies of Jesus that were written rather close to his lifetime, especially by ancient standards. However, the fact that the Gospels were written near the lifetime of Jesus is hardly the only reason why we can be confident that they are useful historical sources for the life of Jesus.

First, the highly respected New Testament scholar Richard Bauckham makes a strong case in his book *Jesus and the Eyewitnesses: The Gospels as Eyewitness Testimony* that we can be quite confident that much of the material in the Gospels comes from people who knew Jesus personally and were familiar with the details of his life and ministry. Bauckham makes the case that the Gospel of Mark (our earliest Gospel, being written only about 30 years or so after Jesus's lifetime) contains considerable eyewitness testimony from Peter who was purportedly one of Jesus's earliest followers.[24] Bauckham notes that

---

24. Richard Bauckham, *Jesus and the Eyewitnesses: The Gospels as Eyewitness Testimony* (Grand Rapids: Eerdmans, 2006), 155-182.

not only does Mark explicitly claim Peter as an eyewitness source, but Peter's perspective also is privileged throughout the Gospel.[25]

To add weight to Bauckham's case, highly respected New Testament scholar Craig Blomberg has made the case that we need not be overly concerned about the gap between Jesus's lifetime and when the Gospels were written. Again, they were written rather close to his lifetime, especially by ancient standards, but they were also written in a highly oral culture where people were used to memorizing whatever information they needed to know.

When was the last time you memorized something in great detail? In Jesus's day, many people memorized the first five books of the Old Testament as well as portions of the prophetic literature and the Psalms. Thus, it is not unreasonable to conclude that Jesus's early followers would have known basic facts about his life and memorized many of his teachings by heart. In this quote, Blomberg gives us valuable insight into the culture during Jesus's day and how memorization of important material was prized. First-century Judaism was an oral culture, steeped in the educational practice of memorization. Some rabbis had the entire Hebrew Scriptures (the Christian Old Testament) committed to memory. Memorizing and preserving intact the amount of information contained in one Gospel would not have been hard for someone raised

---

25. Ibid, 179-180.

in this kind of culture who valued the memories of Jesus's life and teaching as sacred.[26]

From a completely historical perspective, we have good reasons for believing the Gospels are good sources of information for the life of Jesus. Not only were they written close to his lifetime, but professional New Testament scholars have also made the case they contain eyewitness material and were composed in a highly oral culture that would have remembered well the details of Jesus's life and teachings.

Even with this historically approved evidence, it didn't allay all my doubts about Christ and his resurrection. If I was going to claim Christianity as my foundation and live my life for God in the hope of what Jesus Christ had done by rising from the dead, I was going to need a bit more proof that it wasn't just a story. My research continued.

---

26. Craig Blomberg, "The Historical Reliability of the Gospels," North American Mission Board, accessed March 5, 2019, https://www.namb.net/apologetics-blog/the-historical-reliability-of-the-gospels-1/.

# Chapter 8

# THE EXISTENCE OF JESUS

When you are seeking answers to some of life's most challenging questions, you can get downright nitpicky about the details. As I began to look back on what I had learned about Jesus's life during my study, I was beginning to see that the idea that Jesus had never even existed was probably unnecessarily skeptical. Not only do we have the sources of Josephus and Tacitus, but we have four biographies of Jesus that are historically reliable.

With all this in mind it is not hard to see why almost no professional New Testament scholars believe that Jesus was not a historical person.[27] Bart Ehrman represents well the opinion of most professional New Testament scholars when he writes:

> The idea that Jesus did not exist is a modern notion.
> It has no ancient precedents. It was made up in the

_____

27. Licona, *The Resurrection of Jesus: A New Historiographical Approach*, 62-66.

eighteenth century. One might as well call it a modern myth, the myth of the mythical Jesus.[28]

It was a comfort in this journey to find that it was *very reasonable* to conclude that Jesus was a real flesh-and-blood historical figure. Not only that, but there is also strong scholarly consensus on many important facts about his life. New Testament scholar E.P. Sanders makes the case in his book *The Historical Figure of Jesus* that the Gospels are useful sources for the life of Jesus and that there are numerous details about his life that are almost universally accepted as historical by professional scholars of antiquity.

Sanders reports that almost all professional scholars of the New Testament are convinced that Jesus was a historical person, was baptized by John the Baptist, had a ministry in which he preached the "Kingdom of God," had disciples who learned his teachings, that he caused a disturbance in Jerusalem that lead to his arrest by the Jewish authorities, and that he was later put to death by crucifixion on the orders of Pontius Pilate.[29]

Now that I was becoming more acquainted with the historical sources for Jesus's life, I was beginning to see that we know quite a lot about Jesus. Remarkably, discovering this information was already having an impact on

---

28. Bart D. Ehrman, *Did Jesus Exist? The Historical Argument for Jesus of Nazareth* (New York: HarperCollins, 2013), 96.

29. E.P. Sanders, *The Historical Figure of Jesus* (London: Penguin Books, 1995), 10-11.

my faith. Not only was I becoming more confident that God existed, but I was also beginning to know Jesus in a way I had never known him before. This impassioned me to continue this truth journey. More than ever, I had to know the truth for myself, for my family, and for my congregation.

If I asked you about your first memory of hearing the name Jesus, what would it be? See, I don't remember a time when I did not know the name of Jesus of Nazareth. But for me, he had sometimes seemed like an otherworldly figure. Now, I was beginning to see more clearly that Jesus was a historical, flesh-and-blood, Jewish person whom we know a great deal about. We can confirm Jesus's historicity in the same way we confirm the historicity of Alexander the Great and Julius Caesar. Jesus was a real human being, with emotions, with beliefs, with specific ideas about his role in this world and who he was.

So, what did Jesus think about himself?

That was the question I had to answer next. The fact that reliable historical sources attested to Jesus of Nazareth's existence and his crucifixion was certainly helpful in my quest for truth. I could at least begin a thorough investigation into his purported resurrection because I could confirm these other more basic details about his life. Now, I needed to know what Jesus thought about his identity as well as his purpose in life.

If a great moral teacher and charismatic preacher died a brutal death and his followers later claimed he was resurrected, this might be interesting for the historically curious. But even more so, it would be infinitely more significant and life altering if this same great moral teacher and charismatic preacher claimed to be *divine* and speak on behalf of God. Claims to divinity and being God's unique representative to all people are bold claims indeed. If Jesus was lying or was confused about his identity, then it is hard to conceive of God resurrecting him. If God did resurrect him, it was the ultimate stamp of approval on Jesus's teachings and affirmation of who he claimed to be.

Now, in order to understand more clearly who Jesus thought himself to be, it is helpful to understand a little about the culture that Jesus served through his ministry. Jesus lived in Palestine sometime between 5 BCE and 35 CE or so. During this period the Jewish people lived under the dominion of the Roman Empire. Life for a Jew in the Roman Empire was often very difficult. Roman taxes were high, and the authorities ruled with an iron fist. Think IRS, but instead of taking your house, they can kill you if you don't pay your taxes.

During periodic Jewish uprisings, the Romans would execute hundreds of rebels via crucifixion in very public places to quell would-be partisans. Under such difficult conditions, many of the Jewish people began to look back on passages in the Old Testament that spoke of a coming "Messiah" (see Psalm 2, Daniel 7:13-14). If I had lived in those days, I am sure I would be looking for someone who was going to come and save me too! The Jewish people in Jesus's day began to long for a Messiah sent by God himself who would deliver them from Roman dominion and bring spiritual renewal to the people of Israel.

Did Jesus believe that he was the promised Messiah that the Old Testament speaks of? Did he think of himself as sent from God? Christians believe Jesus to be the Messiah, but does the historical record show that Jesus thought of himself in this way?

The answer is yes. Remarkably, we do have some very early evidence that Jesus did think of himself as the Messiah and sent from God to be his authoritative messenger to the world. In Mark 8:27-30, our earliest Gospel written only about 25 to 30 years after Jesus's lifetime and based on even earlier historical sources, we are made aware of a conversation Jesus had with some of his disciples. The text reads:

> Jesus and his disciples went on to the villages around Caesarea Philippi. On the way he asked them, "Who do people say I am?" They replied, "Some say John the Baptist; others say Elijah; and still others, one of the prophets." "But what about you?" he asked. "Who do you say I am?" Peter answered, "You are the Messiah." Jesus warned them not to tell anyone about him.

While it is intriguing that Jesus warns his disciples not to spread the word that he is the Messiah, it is even more curious that he does not correct his disciples on the matter. This strongly implies that he thought of himself as the Messiah. Many scholars of the New Testament are convinced that this passage is probably historical. Not only is it found in the very early source of Mark, but it also accords well with the historical milieu that Jesus was living in. The Jews were on the lookout for a Messiah, and it would not have been strange for them to be discussing this matter and probing whether Jesus was in fact the Messiah. Furthermore, John 6:69 provides another historical source to back up this incident.[30]

Jesus also acted in ways that strongly suggest he thought of himself as the Messiah and God's unique representative to the world. In Mark 11:1-11 we read the story of Jesus riding into Jerusalem on a young donkey just days before his execution. Each account tells us that when he arrived in the city, a crowd gathered around Jesus and began to shout, "Hosanna, blessed is he who comes in the name of the Lord!" Evidently, at least some of the Jewish people were convinced that Jesus was the Messiah and sent from God to minister to them.

Why is this story significant? What does it reveal about Jesus's understanding of himself? It reveals that Jesus thought of himself as the Messiah. Why? He chose to ride into Jerusalem on a young donkey. He was actively trying to fulfill a prophecy about the Messiah we find in Zechariah 9:9 which says "Rejoice greatly, O daughter Zion! Shout aloud, O daughter Jerusalem! Lo, your king comes to you; triumphant and victorious is he, humble and riding on a donkey, on a colt, the foal of a donkey" (NRSV). From this early historical anecdote, we can discern that Jesus now wanted to be identified as the Messiah with the larger Jewish public. Thus, he (very publicly) ful-

---

30. Craig, *On Guard: Defending Your Faith with Reason and Precision*, 198.

filled a well-known prophecy about the coming Messiah that most Jews of the day would have been familiar with.

Some scholars have argued that this story is unhistorical, but eminent philosopher, theologian, and Christian apologist William Lane Craig offers a contrasting perspective:

> Skeptical scholars have sometime questioned the historicity of Jesus' triumphal entry because such a public demonstration would have led to Jesus' immediate arrest by the Romans. But this is a very weak objection. A man on a slowly moving donkey with no show of arms would hardly look menacing. His triumphal entry was not something the Romans were expecting or would have understood, and His procession probably just melted into the crowd once it got to Jerusalem. According to Mark 11:1, upon His arrival Jesus just looks around and then leaves. He does nothing to provoke arrest by the Roman authorities.[31]

Not only does the historical account seem plausible on its face, but the fact that we find it in Mark, our earliest Gospel, further supports the historicity of the incident. Finally, the event is doubly attested in both Mark 11 and John 12, thus further supporting the historical veracity of the event.

It is a lot to take in, but there is even more! We also know from further historical investigation that Jesus

---

31. Craig, *On Guard: Defending Your Faith with Reason and Precision,* 200.

did not think of himself as *just* the Messiah. Rather, he thought of himself as even more than that. The Jews of Jesus's day were convinced that God would send them a *human* deliverer, but as we will see very soon, Jesus did not think of himself as only human. Jesus believed that he was *divine* as well.

Perhaps one of the more revealing passages in the Gospels about what Jesus thought of himself is found in Mark 14:60-64, a very early historical source. In this passage, we find Jesus in the court of the Sanhedrin (the most important religious and legal body of the Jewish people during Jesus's day) on trial for the charge of blasphemy against the God of Israel whom Jesus ostensibly worshipped and served. The text reads:

> Then the high priest stood up before them and asked Jesus, "Are you not going to answer? What is this testimony that these men are bringing against you?" But Jesus remained silent and gave no answer. Again, the high priest asked him, "Are you the Messiah, the Son of the Blessed One?" "I am," said Jesus. "And you will see the Son of Man sitting at the right hand of the Mighty One and coming on the clouds of heaven." The high priest tore his clothes. "Why do we need any more witnesses?" he asked. "You have heard the blasphemy. What do you think?" They all condemned him as worthy of death.

Let me point out a few parts of this scripture passage that deserve mention. First, in the narrative the high priest asks Jesus if he believes himself to be "The Messiah" and "The Son of the Blessed One" or "The Son of God." Jesus responds in the affirmative to both queries by saying "I am" and then goes on to call himself the "Son of Man." Wait a minute, Julian, why would it be important that Jesus affirmed that he was the Messiah, the Son of God, and the Son of Man? For one, we know from earlier, as well as from the passage in question, that Jesus believed himself to be the Messiah which means that he believed he was sent by, and on a mission, from God. Jesus did not merely think of himself as a teacher of ethics and the law, he thought of himself as far more.

Second, Jesus affirming that he was "The Son of Blessed One" or "The Son of God" is a very strong claim when the implications of this title are considered. When Jesus affirmed that he was "The Son of God" he was making the claim that he had a unique "Father/Son" relationship with God that no one else shared. Regarding his sonship, Jesus said radical things such as that God could only be fully and truly known through him (see Luke 10:22).

Finally, we must give attention to Jesus's affirmation that he was "The Son of Man." This was Jesus's favorite title for himself in the Gospels. He refers to himself this way roughly 80 times. What is so interesting about Jesus's favorite title for himself is the fact that he intentionally called himself "*The* Son of Man" rather than simply "*A* Son of Man."

You see, Jewish people sometimes called themselves "*A* Son of Man" to emphasize their humanity. However, the fact that Jesus calls himself "*The* Son of Man" should clue us into the fact that Jesus was trying to say something very different from other Jewish writers. By calling himself "*The* Son of Man," Jesus was saying that he was the fulfillment of the prophecy recorded in Daniel 7:13-14. Let's read it before we dissect it.

> In my vision at night I looked, and there before me was one like a son of man, coming with the clouds of heaven. He approached the Ancient of Days and was led into his presence. He was given authority, glory and sovereign power; all nations and peoples of every language worshiped him. His dominion is an everlasting dominion that will not pass away, and his kingdom is one that will never be destroyed.

By frequently calling himself "The Son of Man," Jesus was trying to clue his Jewish audience into the fact that he believed himself to be the fulfillment of this prophecy. By identifying himself with "The Son of Man" figure in this passage, he is saying that he has the right to be in the presence of the "Ancient of Days" or God himself. He is further making the claim that he is worthy of glory, authority, and rulership. Perhaps most striking of all, he is worthy of *worship*. Considering Jesus's background in strict monotheistic Judaism, this is a bold claim. The text seems to indicate very strongly that Jesus is making a claim to divine status here.

As the fall of 2014 progressed, my research was showing me that we can know a tremendous amount of historical information about Jesus of Nazareth. It was mind blowing, considering that he lived roughly 2,000 years ago. Not only could I rely on the historical sources of Tacitus and Josephus to tell me about Jesus's life, but I also had four historically credible biographies of Jesus of Nazareth in the Gospels. I started this journey wondering if Jesus was real, and through this crisis of faith I could now confirm that Jesus was a real flesh-and-blood person, was baptized by John the Baptist, had a ministry in which he preached the "Kingdom of God," had disciples who learned his teachings, that he caused a disturbance in Jerusalem that led to his arrest by the Jewish authorities, and that he was later put to death by crucifixion on the orders of Pontius Pilate.

Understanding the careful study of the historical sources for Jesus's life reveals someone who thought of himself in ways that strike any thoughtful person as incredible. Jesus was convinced that he was the Jewish Messiah, sent of God, spoke uniquely for God to all people, and was even worthy of worship due to his divine status. If Jesus believed these things about himself and died by crucifixion never to rise again, we could reasonably conclude, as the great author and Christian thinker C.S. Lewis often pointed out, that Jesus was either severely deluded or was simply a deceptive leader of a new religious movement.

What if Jesus believed these things about himself, died from crucifixion, and credible historical evidence supported that he came back to life shortly after his crucifixion? Then this would confirm the truth of what Jesus said and believed about himself. A man who claimed to speak uniquely for God, to provide salvation to all people (not just the Jewish people) and came back to life after a gruesome death is a man who probably deserves our allegiance (to put it rather mildly). However, a major question remained for me: Does the resurrection of Jesus have a strong historical foundation?

To be honest, as I began to thoroughly investigate this question I was sometimes filled with mixed emotions. On the one hand, it was extremely exciting to learn more about who Jesus was than I ever had before. As someone who has always loved history, it was exciting to see that we could investigate Jesus's life using the tools of professional, critical scholars and come away knowing quite a lot about Jesus. However, if the historical evidence did not support Jesus's resurrection, would my faith ever recover?

Looking back from where I stand now, I've come to see that there are many good reasons to be a Christian beyond the evidence for the resurrection of Jesus (though I still think the truth of the resurrection is the best). However, at this stage in my spiritual journey I was truly rebuilding my faith from the ground up. Oftentimes, very little felt certain. The thought of coming this far only to be disappointed greatly depressed me.

For honesty's sake let me say once more that it was my sincere desire that Christianity be proven true. I loved the Christian faith, its history, its worship and liturgy, its diversity, it all fascinated me. I wanted to continue being a part of it all. It would have been very easy for me to abandon my quest and simply believe whatever I wanted to believe. I had a good job working for the church, I could outwardly conform and bury my doubts … perhaps they would eventually go away, and all would be well.

It wasn't good enough for me, and honestly that option shouldn't be good enough for any of us. The truth was worth pursuing despite the emotional, mental, and spiritual toll. My journey had to continue. To investigate the resurrection of Jesus thoroughly I read the work of scholars who believed in its reality as well as the work of skeptical scholars. I continued to view formal debates where both sides were given an opportunity to make their case. I learned more about the resurrection of Jesus than I ever thought I would know. Let me share what I learned with you in the next chapter. The quest continues!

## Chapter 9

# THE HISTORICAL EVIDENCE FOR THE RESURRECTION OF JESUS

My quest for truth had led me to this final destination: Did the available historical evidence support the resurrection of Jesus or not? There could be no peace for me until I could say with confidence, either way. My first stop was a book by William Lane Craig. His book, titled *The Son Rises*, was my first introduction to historical evidence about the resurrection of Jesus.

This wasn't a new book. It had been published for some time and it was essentially a short summation of Craig's doctoral research while he was studying at the University of Munich. For me, the information I found within *The Son Rises* was revolutionary! Never had I heard (or read) someone defend the historical veracity of the resurrection of Jesus so persuasively before. Much less someone with two earned doctorates from two prestigious research universities! However, I also discovered, much to my surprise, just how many faithful Christians with terminal degrees from respected universities had produced admirable defenses of the resurrection of Jesus. Richard Swinburne, Gary Habermas, and Michael Licona (to name just a few) were all respected academics who had done advanced research on, and defended admirably, the historical truth of the resurrection of Jesus.

While I was excited about how many scholars (who had incredible academic backgrounds) believed there was plenty of evidence to support Christ's resurrection, I had to make sure. That meant also investigating the arguments of those who challenged the historicity of the resurrection. Figures such as Bart Ehrman, Shabir Ally (a well-known Muslim apologist), and John Shelby Spong (an Episcopalian churchman, no less!). These experts were all skeptical of the resurrection of Jesus.

This investigation was doing more than leading me to truth. My knowledge of scripture, who Jesus was, and the culture in which he lived was increasing exponentially! The more I read and studied the more I was blown away with just how much we could know about Jesus and his ministry. Don't get me wrong, I still struggled with doubt sometimes, but in all of this searching, my passion to teach the Bible to others was returning. Even increasing. Learning from the world's finest New Testament scholars (both Christian and non-Christian) and coming to know who Jesus was on a deeper and richer level was empowering to my teaching ministry and even more importantly my *faith*.

There was no small amount of excitement at discovering the real flesh-and-blood Jesus who walked the hills of Palestine so long ago, preaching the coming of the kingdom of God. My heart filled with excitement as I began to contemplate the possibility of God dramatically revealing himself in history via the resurrection of Jesus. My hunger for knowledge and truth was ravenous. I could almost see the finish line of my journey and I was more inspired to finish than ever before.

During my research, I discovered that at least three lines of historical evidence support the reality of Christ's resurrection. These three lines of evidence do not exhaust the evidence for the resurrection. However, they are perhaps the most critical to demonstrating that the resurrection of Jesus enjoys strong historical foundation.

First, strong historical evidence supports that Jesus was given an honorable burial in a tomb by an individual named Joseph of Arimathea. Second, strong historical evidence supports that Jesus's tomb was found empty a few days after his death on the cross (his death on the cross being almost universally accepted by professional scholars of the historical Jesus).[32] Third, there is strong historical evidence to support that Jesus of Nazareth's followers saw him alive after his death on the cross.

Now that I have mentioned the lines of evidence that we will examine, a methodological note is in order. The historical sources that support these key aspects of the

---

32. Sanders, *The Historical Figure of Jesus,* 10-11.

resurrection narrative are all found in what is now referred to as the New Testament of the Christian Bible.
Now, I can already hear you coming back at me, "That's
not fair, you can't just appeal to Christianity's sacred book
to prove that the resurrection of Jesus really happened."
To those of you who might be saying this or something
similar right now I want you to know that I take this objection seriously and it deserves a good answer.

While I take this objection seriously, I also believe that
it is ultimately confused. Let me begin my response by
stating unequivocally that I am not about to make the case
that Jesus rose from the dead simply because "the Bible
tells me so," because the Bible is without error, or because
it is God's Word. Such a case would only be convincing to
the Christian, to those who are already convinced. As a
committed Christian I have a very, very high view of the
Bible, believing it to be God's inspired Word, but I don't
argue for the resurrection in this way simply because it's
not very persuasive to the skeptic.

In the following pages I will appeal to many sources
found in the Bible, not as sacred scripture, but as *historical sources*. If you think this is out of bounds, you should
know that many non-Christian biblical scholars (and
they are numerous) regularly mine the Bible for historical
knowledge. Non-Christian scholars such as Bart Ehrman,
Hector Avalos, Gerd Lüdemann, and many others have
no trouble believing that the Bible contains useful historical information about Jesus of Nazareth and the early
Christian community. All of them think it contains historical errors, but it's still a document worthy of serious

historical study. Furthermore, they also believe that by applying the best tools of historical analysis, Bible study can render valuable information about the past.

It should also be remembered that the books that currently make up the New Testament were not always a part of a single, sacred compendium. They were written by a wide variety of different authors, many of whom were eyewitnesses to the ministry of Jesus of Nazareth. Thus, the New Testament should not be viewed as one historical source for the life of Jesus, but rather a compendium that contains many historical sources for the life of Jesus.

Bottom line, just because the New Testament is a sacred book to some, it does not preclude us from studying it as a historian would, mining it for valuable information about the past. Including information about the resurrection of Jesus.

Now some of you might say that this rebuttal just isn't good enough. "I'd like to see non-Christian sources favored over Christian ones." The problem with this argument is that it ignores the fact that the historical sources contained in the many books of the New Testament are by far our earliest and best sources for the life of Jesus. To pass over the historical sources contained in the New Testament in favor of later sources, such as the apocryphal Gospel of Thomas or the Gospel of Peter, would be grotesque historical malpractice. It would be favoring weaker, less reliable sources over inherently stronger and more reliable sources. Summing up, in the following pages I will now investigate the Bible not only as a theologian but as a historian to make a case for the resurrection of

Jesus. For this purpose, the Bible need not be inerrant or inspired by God, it need only contain at least some accurate information about the past.

The first thing I noticed (and it wasn't much of a surprise) was that Jesus's honorable burial in a tomb by Joseph of Arimathea has been challenged by some scholars. Bart Ehrman has questioned this line of evidence's truthfulness in multiple formal debates[33] and John Dominic Crossan (a former Roman Catholic priest turned New Testament scholar) has also questioned it in his book *Who Killed Jesus?* In his writings, Crossan has suggested that it is far more likely that Jesus was buried in a shallow, mass grave with the other criminals rather than given an honorable burial. To add insult to injury, Crossan even speculated that Jesus's body was probably eaten by wild dogs! Crossan's view is shared by some professional scholars of the historical Jesus, and this rebuttal hit my search hard. When seeking truth, we have to look at all sides and sometimes that means considering the possibility that your search for truth may end up where you didn't want to go. Could we give positive reasons for coming to a different conclusion than Crossan and show that Jesus's honorable burial is more likely than what Crossan concludes?

Standing on the edge of truth, I was beginning to see things differently. Not only did I believe there was sub-

---

33. See his debates on Youtube with either William Lane Craig or Michael Licona.

stantial evidence to support Jesus's honorable burial, but I also became convinced that there are several reasons for rejecting Crossan's view.

Let's start at the beginning. First, the story of Jesus's burial by Joseph of Arimathea is attested in Mark 15:42-47. Don't overlook this detail. It is important as Mark is the earliest biography we have of Jesus, having been written sometime around 60 CE. This makes it less likely that the burial account we find in Mark is a later addition to the Jesus story. The fact that Mark was written only 20 to 30 years after Jesus's earthly ministry is impressive enough by ancient standards, but remember that the Gospels are based on reliable oral testimony and even earlier historical sources. Many sources contained within Mark's biography are far older than the work itself and go back to the very earliest days of the Christian movement.

As my research continued, I found the work of German New Testament scholar Rudolph Pesch. He believes that the Passion story of Mark 14-15 dates to much earlier than 60 CE. Pesch is convinced that Mark is not the sole author of the Passion narrative that we see in his Gospel. Instead, he believes Mark borrowed this much earlier source and added it to his Gospel to complete it. Why would Pesch believe that? He is convinced of this because most of Mark's Gospel is composed of anecdotes about Jesus's life and ministry, often with little to connect the events themselves. It is hardly surprising that Mark would borrow from another source and add it to his account of Jesus's life with little editing.

If you sit down and read Mark, you will see his Gospel is not chronological. But when we get to the Passion account, the writing style of the Gospel changes noticeably and we see a cohesive, chronological account that is unlike the rest of his Gospel. Furthermore, in the Passion narrative whenever the high priest[34] is mentioned, his name does not appear. Why is this important? Pesch points out that omitting the name of the high priest suggests that this ancient account was written contemporaneously (or shortly thereafter the events that they record). Naming the high priest would have been pointless to add. When this account was written the high priest Caiaphas (who was instrumental in having Jesus crucified) was probably still in control and thus naming him explicitly was unnecessary. Everyone already knew who he was. William Lane Craig takes Pesch's work and explains it further:

> One of the arguments that Pesch uses is that the pre-Markan passion story never refers to the high priest by name. It just says *the high priest says this or that*, as though I were to say, "The president is holding a dinner at the White House" and everybody would know whom I meant, namely the man currently in power. And since Caiaphas, I think, held the high priesthood until around AD 38 or so, Pesch thinks that this pre-Markan passion story must be an incredibly early source for the final week of Jesus' suffering and death including his burial,

---

34. The high priest was the most important religious official in Israel in Jesus's day and was instrumental in having Jesus crucified.

the discovery of his empty tomb, and the prediction of the postmortem appearances.[35]

Even if you do not find Craig and Pesch's reasoning entirely persuasive on this point, it still must be admitted that we have (in the Gospel of Mark) a rather early source to support the assertion that Jesus of Nazareth was given an honorable burial by Joseph of Arimathea.

As a side note, the burial narrative finds some support in the very early source of 1 Corinthians 15:3-7 which reads:

> For what I received I passed on to you as of first importance: that Christ died for our sins according to the Scriptures, that he was buried, that he was raised on the third day according to the Scriptures, and that he appeared to Cephas, and then to the Twelve. After that, he appeared to more than five hundred of the brothers and sisters at the same time, most of whom are still living, though some have fallen asleep. Then he appeared to James, then to all the apostles.

So far, I have relied on the Gospels and a few other ancient sources (such as Tacitus and Josephus) to provide information about Jesus's life. However, we also have the writings of other early members of the Christian com-

---

35. William Lane Craig and Kevin Harris, "Questions on the Virgin Birth, Bart Ehrman, and Dating the Gospels," Reasonable Faith, accessed June 24, 2019, https://www.reasonablefaith.org/media/reasonable-faith-podcast/questions-on-the-virgin-birth-bart-ehrman-and-dating-the-gospels/.

munity which are useful for historical purposes. Most scholars are convinced that 1 Corinthians 15 was written sometime between 53-54 CE. That would make this source perhaps even older than Mark, depending on which dating model of the Gospels you find most accurate. (It should be noted that a few credible scholars, such as John A.T. Robinson, have dated the Gospel of Mark as early as 45 CE.)

We should also consider the fact that almost all scholars who have studied 1 Corinthians 15:3-7 in detail are convinced that Paul is quoting an even earlier source which he did not author. One that is independent of the Gospels and affirms that Jesus received a decent burial.

The burial narrative is further supported by a unique detail about Joseph of Arimathea that needs to be considered. Mark 15:43 informs us that Joseph of Arimathea was a "prominent member of the Council." The Council being referred to in this passage is likely the Sanhedrin.[36] In Jesus's day, the Sanhedrin was a religious and political body made up of experts on the Hebrew Scriptures (The Old Testament.) The Sanhedrin had great religious and political sway in Jesus's day and the Romans allowed them a wide berth in enforcing the demands of the Mosaic law on the Jewish people.

Most of the members of the Sanhedrin had no love for Jesus. There were a notable few, such as Joseph of

---

36. Craig S. Keener, *The IVP Bible Background Commentary* (Downers Grove, IL; IVP Academic, 2014), 174.

Arimathea, a figure named Nicodemus, and possibly the great teacher of the law Gamaliel, who were sympathetic to Jesus's message. Most members of the Sanhedrin saw Jesus as a heretic, blasphemer, and troublemaker. His influence was widespread, and they very much wanted to see his ministry ended. Even if they had to murder him to get the job done. Eventually, the Sanhedrin managed to convict Jesus in a kangaroo court on trumped up charges and relied upon the Romans to execute him via crucifixion.

Because the Sanhedrin had convicted Jesus so unjustly, the early Christian movement had no love for the Sanhedrin, and with good reason! For them, the Sanhedrin was a mockery of what a deliberative body of holy men should look like. Furthermore, Acts 4:1-22, a relatively early Christian document (written sometime around 70 CE or so), demonstrates that the early Christian community was actively persecuted by the Sanhedrin and that Jesus's early followers openly disregarded their orders against spreading the teachings of Jesus. There was a great deal of animosity between the Sanhedrin and Jesus's earliest followers, and the opinion of the early Christian movement concerning the Sanhedrin was typically negative.

Considering the negative attitude that the early Christian community had toward the Sanhedrin, it is unlikely that the burial narrative in Mark 15 is a later, fictional fabrication. The disdain the early Christian community held towards the Sanhedrin was strong and it is unlikely they would have invented a story about one of its members giving Jesus an honorable burial. The last thing the early Christian community wanted to do was lionize what they saw as a hopelessly corrupt and evil body. This is only one more reason why we can reasonably conclude that the burial narrative is likely authentic.

Now, we have at least two early and independent sources to back up that Jesus was given an honorable burial (see Mark 15 and 1 Corinthians 15). With the evidence at hand, it is very unlikely that the burial account is a fabrication. Scholars such as Ehrman and Crossan have questioned the truthfulness of the burial narrative, but rarely do they give specific arguments to contradict the evidence presented. Indeed, Crossan provides no competing historical sources to support his assertion that Jesus was buried in a shallow mass grave and that his body was eaten by wild animals. Until evidence to the contrary is put forward, we can reasonably conclude that Jesus was given an honorable burial by Joseph of Arimathea in a tomb.

Over the course of 2014 I had learned so much about Jesus of Nazareth. I started this journey with a crisis of faith that had rocked my worldview. I questioned the most basic precepts of the Christian faith, but as this journey of truth continued, it seemed that my faith was slowly being rebuilt. My confidence in God was steadily growing as I continued to study the moral argument and other arguments for the existence of God. God's reality and presence were confirmed to me whenever I reflected on the beauty of the natural world and the apparent design behind the cosmos.

With the basis of my belief in God solidifying, I was building the basis of what I knew about Jesus. Through this journey I now knew that Jesus was a historical, flesh-and-blood person whom we knew much about. I could confidently believe that he existed historically, preached the kingdom of God, claimed to be divine and to speak for God, and that he died by crucifixion sometime between 30 CE and 33 CE. Evidence was presented to me through my research that there was good historical evidence that Jesus was given an honorable burial by Joseph of Arimathea.

However, the real test of whether Christianity was true was now directly in my sight. The truth of the empty tomb and the validity of the resurrection appearances to the early Christian community were the pillars upon which the case for the resurrection of Jesus stood or fell.

Would the evidence for the empty tomb and the resurrection appearances be as strong as the evidence for Jesus's burial or his crucifixion? Jesus claimed very strong things about himself. He claimed to forgive sins and to be the Savior of the world; he even claimed to be divine. If he did not rise from the dead, then he was deluded or deceptive. However, if he did rise again, then clearly his claims about himself can reasonably be trusted and accepted.

Admittedly, when studying the evidence for the empty tomb and Jesus's resurrection appearances, I was filled with a little trepidation and worry. Would the evidence be up to snuff? Is this where the case would fall apart? There were still some times when I considered abandoning my quest and retreating into the subjective. Could I enjoy the cultural and social benefits of Christianity (still considerable in some parts of the American South where I live) without being sure of its truthfulness? Maybe some could, but I knew I would never have peace if I concluded my research at this juncture. I needed to know that what I believed was true. In 2014, I vividly remember praying fervently, even desperately, to God for hours to show me the truth, to reveal himself to me, to not allow me to accept easy answers. Instead, I committed to pursuing the truth at all costs. Now was not the time to take the easy road. It was time to continue on the narrow road that leads to truth.

# Chapter 10

# FINDING TRUTH

Truth is rarely easy to come by and the amount of soul searching you undertake in a journey like this one can exhaust you. Throughout this season of doubt, I continued to participate in spiritual disciplines that went beyond prayer and Bible reading. I sought the spiritual and transcendent even as I grappled with doubts about the truth of the Christian faith. I am convinced that every Christian should continue in spiritual disciplines even through their doubts. It is something that can bring peace into the jumbled chaos we are sorting through. I continued to listen to the music of Christian artists such as Michael Card, John Michael Talbot, and Matt Redman. In my darkest moments, I would often listen to Matt Redman's song "10,000 Reasons (Bless the Lord)." Headphones in, I would play it repeatedly and allow the simple chords and lyrics (taken directly from the Bible) to minister to my hurting soul. It was in those moments that I realized the beautiful can sometimes point to greater realities beyond us. Prayer and music sustained my faith when I could not answer every question. Despite staying fervent in my spiritual disciplines, I still needed to know if the Christian worldview was true. I needed to know that Jesus's tomb was found empty and that his disciples had experienced him after his death on the cross. My quest had to continue.

During my research, I discovered the work of philosopher and New Testament scholar Gary Habermas. Habermas is quite possibly the world's greatest living scholar on the resurrection of Jesus of Nazareth. Not only was it the subject of his doctoral dissertation but he has continued to do top-notch research on the subject until the present day. As I was studying the evidence for the empty tomb, I discovered an article he had written called "Resurrection Research from 1975 to the Present: What are the critical scholars saying?" He had published this article in 2005. Although by the time of this book's publication this resource will be some 15 years old, I knew that this resource would help me tremendously to visualize the trends in resurrection research in the recent past and to get a good feel on where the scholarly community stood on this area of historical study.

Habermas's study surveyed almost all the scholarly literature in English, French, and German (the world's most important research languages) that pertained to the resurrection of Jesus written between 1975 and 2005. All the literature included in the study was written by people with terminal degrees. In layman's terms, a terminal degree is the highest achievable degree in an academic field or professional discipline.

Add to their credentials the fact that the literature was written by people with very divergent worldviews, and you have an incredible wealth of some serious scholars. Some were conservative Evangelicals while others were liberal or more moderate scholars. Some were atheists and agnostics. The most important part I noted that I want you to take away from this is that many scholars from non-Christian backgrounds were represented in the study too.

Remarkably, Habermas's article reports that an impressive 75 percent of these scholars who had studied the truthfulness of the empty tomb account were convinced that it is historically probable that Jesus's tomb was discovered empty shortly after his death on the cross![37] Although Habermas's paper was already growing older by the time I read it, I knew that many of the people who had written work that was surveyed in his paper were still working in the scholarly guild. The view that there was strong historical evidence to support the empty tomb was not a fringe view. It was supported by numerous professional New Testament scholars and historians of antiquity.

However, with Habermas's work growing older, I knew I could not stop there. Much like the evidence for Jesus's

---

37. Gary R. Habermas, "Resurrection Research from 1975 to the Present: What Are Critical Scholars Saying?," *Faculty Publications and Presentations.* Paper 9. (2005): http://digitalcommons.liberty.edu/sor_fac_pubs/9.

honorable burial, we find substantial historical support for the empty tomb. This detail is found within Mark's Gospel (specifically Mark 16:1-8) that we discussed earlier. Remember, Mark is the earliest of our Gospels and it is based on even earlier, reliable sources such as oral traditions about Jesus as well as the Passion narrative that Mark likely borrowed from someone else. However, Mark is not our only historically credible source to support Jesus's tomb being found empty shortly after his crucifixion.

We can also lean on the Gospel of Matthew as a source for the empty tomb. It must be noted that often the Gospel of Matthew is heavily dependent on the Gospel of Mark for its historical information. Sometimes it quotes Mark's Gospel verbatim. As with any study with multiple sources, we need to be careful. We can't simply make the blanket statement that Mark and Matthew are independent sources from one another. Sometimes they are, and sometimes they are not.

In Matthew 27-28 it is probable that Matthew is working from a source independent of Mark because he provides for us details that Mark does not. Matthew tells us that the Sanhedrin posted guards at the tomb to remove the possibility of anyone stealing the body of Jesus. To point out even more differences, Matthew relates that the explanation circulating among the Jews about Jesus's empty tomb was that his disciples stole his body.

When we include these two details, we can reasonably conclude that Matthew is working from a source independent of Mark. Thus, we have at least two early and independent sources to support that Jesus's tomb was found empty. Historians of antiquity will typically say that an event is highly likely if two independent sources can be produced to support an event. Interestingly, some scholars are convinced we have as many as six early and independent sources to support the empty tomb.[38] For these reasons, it is not hard to see why so many scholars from so many diverse backgrounds are convinced that the fact of the empty tomb enjoys substantial historical support.

Perhaps the best defense of the empty tomb is if it were not true it would have been quite easy for Jesus's opponents to prove its falsity. They could have easily rolled away the stone and put an end to the outrageous tale. Due to the brute fact of the existence of the Christian movement, almost all scholars of antiquity are convinced that at least some of Jesus's early followers believed in Christ's resurrection and began to tell others about it. If the disciples began to preach that Jesus had risen again, with his body still in the tomb, the early Christian movement would have never gotten off the ground.

In Jesus's day, the Jewish people believed that when resurrection took place, the human body *itself* was revived and made new. Leaving no body behind. Resurrection while the body still lay in the tomb would have been an absurdity to the Jews of Jesus's day. If the disciples of Christ began to preach that he had risen again while his body was still in the tomb, the members of the Sanhedrin

---

38. Craig, *Reasonable Faith: Christian Truth and Apologetics,* 366.

and others opposing Jesus could have quickly pointed this out for all to see and squelched the Christian movement forever.

When looking at the facts, we must always look not only to those whose testimony supports what we want, but also at those who oppose it. A few critics have suggested that the empty tomb could be explained away by assuming Jesus's early followers visited the wrong tomb and, noticing the body was not there, believed what Christ had told them and concluded that he had risen again. However, if Jesus's burial by Joseph of Arimathea and his membership within the Sanhedrin are reasonably secure facts (historically speaking), then anyone with a misunderstanding of the where the donated tomb was could have questioned Joseph about the true location.

There is no historical evidence to support the idea that the location of the tomb was not generally well known or reasonably locatable. With guards standing watch, the location need not be in question. With this evidence, a good historical argument can be made in favor of the empty tomb account.

As I began closing in on more and more evidence of the empty tomb, I will admit to the growth of my hope. My heart still wanted this journey to lead me to a place of renewed Christian faith. Each new piece of evidence just provoked me further into seeking the whole truth. We were almost there.

# Chapter 11

# EXPERIENCING JESUS

Have you ever felt as though you were on the precipice of a grand revelation? As I began to approach the final stages of this journey, those beginning moments of this crisis of faith replayed in my mind. Despite the hope that had begun to grow within me, I was faced with tremendous fear about how this journey would end. Would I find substantial information to prove the resurrection was true or would this journey end with more questions than answers? There was no time to lose. It was time to learn the truth.

As I mulled over the honorable burial of Jesus of Nazareth by Joseph of Arimathea and Jesus's tomb being found empty shortly after his death by crucifixion, I began to consider the evidence for the resurrection appearances of Jesus to his early followers. What might surprise you (as it did me) is how many professional scholars (who are deeply familiar with New Testament studies) are convinced that Jesus's early followers experienced him in some way shortly after his crucifixion.

E.P. Sanders, a highly respected New Testament scholar, can be quoted as saying, "That Jesus' followers (and later Paul) had resurrection experiences is, in my judgement, a fact. What the reality was that gave rise to the experiences I do not know."[39] While it should be noted that Sanders is not ready to say as a *scholar* and *historian* that God raised Jesus from the dead, he is quite confident and ready to affirm, along with many other professional New Testament scholars, that Jesus's disciples were thoroughly convinced they saw Jesus alive shortly after his death.

When we consider the number of early and independent sources we have that attest to Jesus's early followers seeing him alive after his death, it is not hard to see why so many professional scholars of the New Testament are quite comfortable concluding that Jesus's early followers experienced him in some way after his death. Indeed, after exhaustively surveying the scholarly literature on the purported resurrection appearances of Jesus, Mike Licona has argued in his important book *The Resurrection of Jesus: A New Historiographical Approach* that almost all scholars have concluded that the disci-

---

39. Sanders, *The Historical Figure of Jesus,* 280.

ples having resurrection experiences of Jesus is a historical fact.[40]

Indeed, the influential Lutheran theologian and historian Wolfhart Pannenberg is convinced that 1 Corinthians 15:3-7, which we discussed earlier, is the earliest and best historical source to support that Jesus's earliest followers experienced him after his death by crucifixion. Pannenberg points out that 1 Corinthians is almost certainly older than the Gospels and that in 1 Corinthians 15:3-7 Paul is quoting a very early tradition which he did not write.

In 1 Corinthians 15:3-7 we are told that many early Christians, including Paul himself, Peter, the Twelve (a group of Jesus's core early followers), and about 500 other people had experiences of Jesus after his death. If we allow that Jesus's earthly ministry concluded sometime around 33 CE, and that the tradition Paul quotes in 1 Corinthians was written sometime before 55 CE (when most scholars think the majority of 1 Corinthians was written), then we have in the 1 Corinthians 15:3-7 text a source going back to within at least 10 or 15 years of Jesus's lifetime attesting to his being seen after his death by his earliest disciples. In reference to the 1 Corinthians 15 text, Pannenberg soberly states:

> In view of the age of the formulated traditions used by Paul and of the proximity of Paul to the

---

40. Licona, *The Resurrection of Jesus: A New Historiographical Approach*, 463-464.

events, the assumption that appearances of the resurrected Lord were really experienced by a number
of members of the primitive Christian community
and not perhaps freely invented in the course of
later legendary development has good historical
foundation.[41]

Pannenberg makes clear that the 1 Corinthians text
was written so near to the time of the events that they
describe, that unless we can provide compelling reasons
to distrust the account, we can reasonably conclude it is a
*reliable, historical* account that attests that many people in
the early Christian community experienced Jesus in some
way after his death.

However, the 1 Corinthians 15 account is hardly the
only early and reliable account that we have that supports the resurrection appearances of Jesus. We read in
Matthew 28:1-10 that it was a group of women who were
the first witnesses to the empty tomb and the first to experience him after his death. This historical anecdote is
further supported by the very early source of Mark 16.

The Matthew 28 source may be the most remarkable
of the appearance anecdotes for a very interesting reason.
To understand why, we need to know a little about Jewish
culture in Jesus's day. During Jesus's day, Jewish culture
was thoroughly patriarchal and there was a decidedly
negative attitude toward women's intellectual abilities as

---

41. Wolfhart Pannenberg, *Jesus-God and Man* (Philadelphia: The
Westminster Press, 1977), 91.

well as their capacity for moral and spiritual virtue. Even at criminal trials in Jesus's day, the testimony of a woman was sometimes declared inadmissible simply on the basis of their sex.

Thus, it is remarkable that Matthew 28 records that it was women who were the first witnesses to the empty tomb and were the first people to see Jesus after his death on the cross. Early pagan critics would seize upon this anecdote to ridicule the early Christian movement. Living in the second century, Greek philosopher Celsus wrote (rather misogynistically) that Christianity was a radical cult started by a group of hysterical women! If the early Christian community had desired to fabricate an account to make the resurrection account more plausible to those outside the early Christian community, then forging an anecdote about women being the first individuals to see Jesus alive would have been the worst way to go about it, at least by ancient standards.

If the early Christian community had wanted to fabricate an ostensibly more culturally palatable account about Jesus's resurrection appearances, they could have said that Jesus's disciples like Peter or John, or even his enemies, had seen him first. For this reason, we can reasonably conclude that the anecdote of women being the first people to see Jesus alive after his death is not a fabrication and is likely historical.

However, these sources are hardly the only two that back up the third line of evidence for Jesus's resurrection. The Gospels are full of other early and independent sources that attest to people seeing Jesus alive soon after his death on the cross. We have evidence that James (the brother of Jesus who was quite skeptical of his brother's ministry early in his life), the disciples on the way to Emmaus, as well as numerous other unnamed people experienced Jesus in some sense shortly after his death on the cross.

With the literal wealth of historical sources that we have at our disposal to verify that the early Christian community believed they saw Jesus after his death, it is not hard to see why even the very skeptical New Testament scholar Gerd Ludemann concludes, "It may be taken as historically certain that Peter and the disciples had experiences after Jesus' death in which Jesus appeared to them as the risen Christ."[42]

After reading a glut of books on New Testament studies and studying the Gospel accounts closely, more often than not, many professional New Testament scholars from a variety of backgrounds were convinced that Jesus is a historically accessible figure. Almost all were convinced that he lived early in the first century, was a charismatic preacher and teacher, and that he was put to death via crucifixion sometime around 33 CE.

Other facts, though somewhat more contested in academic circles, were also defended by many respected scholars in the field, such as the abundance of evidence that Jesus saw himself as the Jewish Messiah, thought of

---

42. Craig, *Reasonable Faith: Christian Truth and Apologetics*, 381.

himself as divine, and claimed to speak for God and with considerable authority. Finally, I learned that the three primary lines of evidence for Jesus's resurrection—namely, his burial by Joseph of Arimathea, the empty tomb, and his appearances to his early followers after his death—all enjoyed strong historical foundation.

However, it was also abundantly clear that even though many scholars were convinced of the historicity of the facts I listed above, they were still skeptical that Jesus was supernaturally raised from the dead by God himself. That very skepticism was still pushing against my faith. The question of "How do we explain these facts?" was still open. Interestingly, many scholars, taking the lead of E.P. Sanders, simply expressed agnosticism as to what to do with the facts surrounding Jesus's purported resurrection. Some, however, tried to offer naturalistic explanations of the data supporting Jesus's resurrection.

However, is it also possible that Jesus was who he said he was, is divine, is the Savior of the world, is worthy of our trust and belief? That God placed his ultimate stamp of approval upon him by raising him from the dead? Is a supernatural explanation the best explanation?

Almost since the beginning of the Christian movement there have been attempts to explain away Jesus's resurrection naturalistically. Perhaps one of the oldest explanations is that Jesus's disciples stole his body from the tomb, left it empty, and then proceeded to spread the message that he had risen again. This objection can be done away with rather quickly as it ignores all the evidence we have about how the early Christian community came to sincerely believe that they had seen Jesus alive in many different instances.

Most scholars find it very unlikely that the disciples created a conspiracy by stealing the body of Jesus then spreading the word that he had risen again. There is simply too much positive evidence in favor of their genuine belief in his resurrection to posit that they cooked up a grand lie. Even more so, we know that at least some of Jesus's disciples died (James was beheaded) or were severely persecuted (Paul and John) for their belief in the resurrection. Would they face death and torture for something they knew to be a lie?

Another naturalistic explanation that I came across in my studies is what is sometimes called the "Apparent Death Theory." This theory was originally suggested by the father of liberal Christian theology Friedrich Schleiermacher in the nineteenth century. Schleiermacher suggested that when Jesus was taken down from the cross, he was near death and unconscious, but the Romans who oversaw his crucifixion had failed to finish him off before they removed his body from the cross. Being unconscious and thought dead by his early followers, he was laid in the tomb only to revive after they left. Thus, being revived, Jesus exited the tomb and presented himself as the risen Lord to his followers.

Even in the midst of my searching for truth, I realized that this explanation suffered on multiple levels. First, it ignores the fact that the Romans were expert executioners who would have never allowed for an error of such magnitude to take place on their watch. Those who experienced the full regimen of the grueling punishment of crucifixion, as Jesus did, simply did not live to tell the tale. Even if we allow that Jesus could have survived crucifixion, which is extremely unlikely, it is even more unlikely that he could have escaped from the tomb in such a weakened state with the presence of guards. Tombs in Jesus's day were typically caves with large stone doors that could only be removed by multiple strong men. It is highly unlikely that Jesus could have overcome such an obstacle and even less likely that he could have overcome the guards who awaited him outside.

The most fatal problem with the "Apparent Death Theory" is that even if Jesus had managed to escape the tomb, he would have never been able to convince his disciples in his severely weakened and injured state that he had experienced resurrection. Again, knowing a little about Jewish religion in Jesus's day is extremely helpful in understanding why the "Apparent Death Theory" is implausible.

Jewish theologians in Jesus's day who believed in the concept of resurrection (some Jewish theologians in Jesus's day, such as the Sadducees, were skeptical of miracles in general and thus thought the concept of resurrection absurd) understood it as not only being brought back to life but also being brought into a completely higher plane of existence. According to the Jews, to be resurrected meant that your body had been cured and delivered from all wounds and disease; furthermore, it was a glorious and radiant body fit for heaven and God's presence. A Jesus who was bloodied and weak due to his experience of crucifixion would not have been able to convince his followers that he had experienced resurrection. His disciples might have been rallied by the fact that he had *survived* the process of crucifixion and successfully resisted the wicked Sanhedrin, but they would not have concluded that he had experienced resurrection.

Objections such as the "Wrong Tomb Theory," which was very briefly discussed earlier, the "Conspiracy Theory" and "Apparent Death Theory" are not as popular as they used to be and are not suggested by very many professional scholars any longer. However, one naturalistic explanation that continues to be popular among some scholars is the theory that Jesus's resurrection appearances can all be explained away by hallucinations. This is the explanation forwarded by prominent New Testament scholar Gerd Lüdemann. With my faith growing and yet teetering on the edge of finding truth I could hear myself asking, *Does this explanation have any merit?*

As I continued my research, I came across at least two major objections that can be levelled against the "Hallucination Hypothesis." While the "Hallucination Hypothesis" can apparently explain the resurrection appearances of Jesus to his earliest followers, it cannot explain why his tomb was found empty. To explain away the empty tomb and make the "Hallucination Hypothesis" work, we will have to rely on one of the other naturalistic, and rather flimsy, explanations covered earlier. In my opinion, this other explanation severely damages the credibility of the "Hallucination Hypothesis."

First, if we were to suggest that the empty tomb can be explained by Jesus's disciples stealing his body from the tomb, this would almost certainly rule out hallucinations as an explanation for his appearances to his earliest followers. Why so? It seems unlikely that the early Christian community would have come to *sincerely* believe that Jesus had risen again since they had so recently handled his lifeless body.

Even if they did have visionary experiences of him after stealing his body away from the tomb, it is more likely that they would have concluded that these experiences were confirmation that Jesus was in God's presence because of his righteous life, not that he had experienced resurrection. Of course, you could suggest the "Wrong Tomb Theory" to explain away the evidence for the empty tomb, but my research had already determined that such an explanation is unlikely.

It seems to me that if you want to make the "Hallucination Hypothesis" work, you have to refute the abundance of evidence for the honorable burial of Jesus by Joseph of Arimathea, thus eliminating the possibility of a tomb being found empty at all. Furthermore, you would have to show that the empty tomb is a later legendary development.

Unfortunately for the "Hallucination Hypothesis," evidence for Jesus's honorable burial and the empty tomb both present with strong historical support. For me, the major problem with the "Hallucination Hypothesis" is that it begs the question by failing to account for Jesus's honorable burial by Joseph of Arimathea and for the fact that Jesus's tomb was found empty shortly after his death. I knew to find the truth I needed things to line up and, thus far, these explanations attempting to explain away the risen Jesus failed to hold water under careful scrutiny.

The "Hallucination Hypothesis" suffers from the fact that we have several early sources (namely 1 Corinthians 15 and Matthew 28) that tell us that Jesus was seen alive by groups of people. Why is this significant? It is significant because most clinical psychologists, psychiatrists, and other mental-health professionals remain skeptical about the possibility of groups of people experiencing a hallucination common to all of them. Those who have studied hallucinations professionally tend to believe that hallucinations are an *individual* phenomenon and not a group phenomenon. Consider the words of licensed clinical psychologist Gary A. Sibcy:

> I have surveyed the professional literature (peer-reviewed journal articles and books) written by psychologists, psychiatrists, and other relevant health-care professionals during the past two decades and have yet to find a single documented case of a group hallucination, that is, an event for which more than one person purportedly shared in a visual or other sensory perception where there was clearly no external referent.[43]

---

43. Licona, *The Resurrection of Jesus: A New Historiographical Approach*, 484.

While the "Hallucination Hypothesis" might be able to explain how individuals could hallucinate about seeing the risen Jesus, it cannot explain the phenomenon of groups of people having resurrection experiences of Jesus as there is little evidence that group hallucinations are even possible.

We also have early evidence that people like Paul, a skeptic of Jesus's ministry, claimed to see Jesus alive. He persecuted the early Christian movement, and it seems unlikely that Paul, considering his disdain for Jesus and his early followers, would hallucinate and see *Jesus of Nazareth* of all people.[44]

The evidence seems to suggest that *most*, if not the vast majority, of Jesus's disciples (and even a few skeptics like James and Paul) came to sincerely believe that he had risen again, and it seems quite implausible to claim that the early Christian community hallucinated en masse and therefore came to believe that Jesus of Nazareth had risen again. If one, or just a few, members of the early Christian community claimed to see Jesus alive, then the "Hallucination Hypothesis" might become suddenly more plausible. However, such does not seem to be the case. Rather, it seems that the majority of Jesus's earliest followers came to believe sincerely in his resurrection. Explaining this via mass hallucinations seems rather impossible.

---

44. For those unfamiliar with Paul's biography, prior to his conversion experience, he was a persecutor of the early Christian community.

So, if naturalistic explanations for Jesus's resurrection do not adequately explain the historical evidence we have—namely, that Jesus of Nazareth was given an honorable burial by Joseph of Arimathea, that his tomb was found empty shortly after his death on the cross, and that he was seen alive by his earliest followers shortly after his death on the cross—how are we to explain what actually took place?

One could simply claim agnosticism, say that the events defy explanation, and that what took place during the earliest days of the Christian movement is one of history's great mysteries. Some New Testament scholars, historians, and other students of the resurrection narratives have come to this conclusion. This would be the easiest way out and don't think that many times during this journey I didn't consider the possibility. I could continue serving in the church and teaching from the Bible, a book I believed to  contain much valuable historical information, and no one would be the wiser. But it just simply would not suffice for me.

Taking a moment to gather all of this evidence that months and months of research had provided, I knew there was a better way to explain the data. If a perfectly moral, all-loving, all-powerful God exists, then the possibility of miracles should not be casually and quickly dismissed. If there is good historical evidence to back up the central lines of evidence that support the resurrection and we can make a reasonable argument for the existence of God, are we not justified in humbly and reasonably concluding that God has revealed himself to us powerfully through Jesus of Nazareth's resurrection?

This journey for truth had led me to one powerful conclusion. It seems to me that only the supernatural explanation—namely, that God raised Jesus of Nazareth from the dead—adequately accounts for all the data. It easily explains the evidence for the empty tomb and Jesus's appearances to his earliest followers without ignoring, or forcing, any of the historical evidence. Such an explanation cannot be quickly set aside, for a good argument can be made that God exists. Thus, Christianity's two most central tenets can be defended cogently and rationally. Christianity is not based on sentimentalism; rather, it is a perfectly rational response of faith based on what experience and history tell us. If this is true, then it has radical and important implications not just for me in finding sure footing after my own crisis of faith, but for *everyone*.

# Epilogue

As is probably no surprise to you, this intellectual and spiritual journey had made me into a very different individual from the one I was before. Remarkably, despite how painful the experience was of nearly losing my faith in 2014, in time my faith would emerge much stronger. I had discovered that the Christian tradition was intellectually and spiritually richer than I had believed before this journey began. As a result of this journey, I learned that when weighty objections are levelled against the Christian faith, we need not retreat to sentimentalism or anti-intellectual responses to retain our beliefs. The Christian faith is well situated to handle the questions of skeptics. There are good reasons for believing there is a God and that Jesus experienced resurrection shortly after his death by crucifixion.

As a result of my spiritual quest, I emerged a more thoughtful person and a better listener, a skill well suited for a pastor. Instead of starting off with a bulletproof faith from childhood, I now knew what it is like to doubt, to struggle, to wonder if anything you believe is really true. When people tell me they are struggling in their faith and that all they want are thoughtful answers or directions to find truth, I understand. Perhaps surprisingly to some, I think my crisis of faith made me a much better pastor and theologian.

When you embark on a journey of this magnitude, many things change. Perhaps the most noticeable change for me came in the way I looked at life itself. Now when I watch my rapidly growing children playing in the front yard, fascinated by the butterflies and the setting sun, I am more confident than ever that the things of nature they so enjoy were created by a morally perfect, all-loving, all-powerful God.

The God who created these wonderful things loves my children and gave us his Son, Jesus of Nazareth, so that everyone might believe in him and experience eternal life. Because there is a God, and Jesus is who he says he is, their lives matter, all people matter, life has meaning, immortality is not a pipe dream. Jesus has proven that immortality is a possibility for all people by rising again. He has proven that death is no challenge to God.

Truth changes all things and through it I had been given a new purpose in life. The wisdom I gained throughout 2014 and 2015 so radically changed me that I had to share this information with others. Thus in 2015, I left the church I had been ordained in and started Risen Savior Ministries, a non-profit dedicated to sharing the message of the Christian faith. I wanted to share what I had learned with as many people as possible. That meant stepping down from pastoral ministry for a little while.

Now that you have heard what it meant for my life to discover that the Christian faith is rational and comes with historical evidence backed by scholars, I invite you to ask yourself this question: "What does this mean for my life?" The Christian tradition is intellectually and spiritually a rich one and I hope that this journey of truth has inspired curiosity in you to seek deeper meaning in these intimate places of your life. God is ready to answer your toughest questions. Jesus is ready to be the unchanging rock you so desperately need in the ever-changing world in which we live.

My only prayer in sharing this journey with you is that it has convinced you to consider the claims of Jesus of Nazareth. Namely, that he is "The Way, The Truth, and The Life" and if you will believe in him and follow him, you can have eternal life. We do not have to fear death any longer because of Jesus's own death, burial, and resurrection. One day we will be resurrected just as he was when he returns and brings history to its climactic end. Because of Jesus, death has been defeated, *decisively*.

Knowing what I do about the world and about my own crisis of faith, it is possible you have not been convinced by my little book. That is OK! I meant what I said in the very beginning. My book is more likely the launching pad for your intellectual and spiritual journey and probably not the destination. If you still have more questions, want to learn more arguments for God's existence (and there are many more), and need to study the evidence for the resurrection of Jesus more thoroughly, then I encourage you to consult the "For Further Reading" section that I have provided at the back of this book. In it, you will find resources written by far more accomplished Christian scholars than myself. I am confident that their work will be able to help you with your questions.

No matter what, keep searching for truth. Consider the possibility that whenever you are compelled to search for what is true, you are actually being led by God himself to do so. God wants a relationship with you, and he wants to satisfy you intellectually and spiritually. He wants to give you peace. Perhaps the greatest thing I gained from my intellectual and spiritual journey is just that, peace.

I now move forward in life more confident than ever that there is a God and that he has revealed himself to us most decisively in the person of Jesus of Nazareth. Confidence in these two facts give me the strength I need to continue in this ever-changing and often frightening world. As a result of my intellectual and spiritual journey, God has given me answers, peace, and most importantly *himself.* Keep searching for God, and I am confident that you will find the abundant life, that I myself have found, in following Jesus of Nazareth.

# Bibliography

Baggett, David and Jerry L. Walls. *Good God: The Theistic Foundations on Morality.* New York: Oxford University Press, 2011.

Bauckham, Richard. *Jesus and the Eyewitnesses: The Gospels as Eyewitness Testimony.* Grand Rapids: Eerdmans, 2006.

Blomberg, Craig. "The Historical Reliability of the Gospels," North American Mission Board, accessed March 5, 2019, https://www.namb.net/apologetics-blog/the-historical-reliability-of-the-gospels-1/.

Craig, William Lane. *On Guard: Defending Your Faith with Reason and Precision.* Colorado Springs: David C. Cook, 2010.

——— *Reasonable Faith: Christian Truth and Apologetics.* Wheaton: Crossway, 2008.

——— *The Son Rises: The Historical Evidence for the Resurrection of Jesus.* Eugene: Wipf and Stock, 2001.

——— "The Problem of Evil," Reasonable Faith, accessed September 19, 2022, https://www.reasonablefaith.org/writings/popular-writings/existence-nature-of-god/the-problem-of-evil/.

——— "Navigating Sam Harris' *The Moral Landscape*," Reasonable Faith, accessed June 24, 2019, https://www.reasonablefaith.org/writ-

ings/popular-writings/existence-nature-of-god/
navigating-sam-harris-the-moral-landscape/.

——— and Kevin Harris, "Questions on the Virgin Birth,
Bart Ehrman, and Dating the Gospels," Reasonable Faith,
accessed June 24, 2019, https://www.reasonablefaith.org/
media/reasonable-faith-podcast/questions-on-the-virgin-
birth-bart-ehrman-and-dating-the-gospels/.

Ehrman, Bart D. *Did Jesus Exist? The Historical Argument
for Jesus of Nazareth.* New York: HarperCollins, 2013.

——— *Jesus, Interrupted: Revealing the Hidden
Contradictions in the Bible (And Why We Don't Know About
Them).* New York: HarperCollins, 2010.

Habermas, Gary R. "Resurrection Research from 1975 to
the Present: What Are Critical Scholars Saying?," *Faculty
Publications and Presentations.* Paper 9. (2005): http://digi-
talcommons.liberty.edu/sor_fac_pubs/9.

Harris, Sam. *The Moral Landscape: How Science Can
Determine Human Values.* New York: Free Press, 2010.

Howell, Martha and Walter Prevenier. *From Reliable
Sources: An Introduction to Historical Methods.* Ithaca:
Cornell University Press, 2001.

Lewis, C.S. *Mere Christianity.* New York: Touchstone, 1996.

Licona, Michael R. *The Resurrection of Jesus: A New
Historiographical Approach.* Downers Grove, IL: IVP
Academic, 2010.

Pannenberg, Wolfhart. *Jesus-God and Man.* Philadelphia:
The Westminster Press, 1977.

Phillips, J.B. *Your God is Too Small.* New York: Macmillan, 1979.

Qureshi, Nabeel. *Seeking Allah, Finding Jesus: A Devout Muslim Encounters Christianity.* Grand Rapids: Zondervan, 2014.

Sanders, E.P, *The Historical Figure of Jesus.* London: Penguin Books, 1995.

# For Further Reading

Craig, William Lane. *On Guard: Defending Your Faith with Reason and Precision*. Colorado Springs: David C. Cook, 2010.

——— *Reasonable Faith: Christian Truth and Apologetics*. Wheaton: Crossway, 2008.

Lewis, C.S. *Mere Christianity*. New York: Touchstone, 1996.

Licona, Michael R. *The Resurrection of Jesus: A New Historiographical Approach*. Downers Grove, IL: IVP Academic, 2010.

Qureshi, Nabeel. *Seeking Allah, Finding Jesus: A Devout Muslim Encounters Christianity*. Grand Rapids: Zondervan, 2014.

# About the Author

Julian Pace is a Christian pastor and author. He currently serves as the Pastor of Central Alliance Church in Mt. Airy, Ga. He is also the President of Risen Savior Ministries a non-profit Christian ministry dedicated to evangelism and church renewal. Julian is the author of more than a dozen popular and scholarly articles that have all been featured in a variety of Christian publications. Julian's writing is fueled by the deeply held conviction that authentic fulfillment is found only in an intimate relationship with Jesus of Nazareth, the Son of God. When Julian is not preaching, teaching, or writing you may find him singing, playing one of his beloved acoustic guitars, or spending time with his family. Julian holds an MA in Biblical Studies from Piedmont International University (now Carolina University) and is currently pursuing a ThD with a focus in Historical Theology from Evangelical Seminary in Myerstown, PA.